The
Yin Yang
Complex

The
Yin Yang
Complex

Create success by understanding
the world's oldest dynamic forces

BRENDAN FOLEY

MERCIER PRESS
IRISH PUBLISHER – IRISH STORY

MERCIER PRESS
Cork
www.mercierpress.ie

Trade enquiries to CMDBookSource,
55a Spruce Avenue, Stillorgan Industrial Park,
Blackrock, County Dublin

© Brendan Foley, 2010

ISBN: 978 1 85635 652 7

10 9 8 7 6 5 4 3 2 1

For Sarah

A CIP record for this title is available from the British Library

Printed and bound in the EU.

Contents

Preface

Joining the Dots

The preface of this book has perhaps been the most difficult section for me to write. The reason for this, as most of you may know, is that it can often be easier to tell someone else's story than to tell your own. What you will read in the coming chapters are my thoughts, beliefs and observations in relation to the balance of masculine (yang) and feminine (yin) energies in their various guises. However, to give you some perspective on where I am coming from, and to help make what you read more tangible, an insight into my own background is necessary.

I think this preface has proved challenging for me to write because it is my truth. I am shedding both my ego and my mask and putting myself at your mercy. But by making myself vulnerable in this way, I have the complete freedom to tell my story.

My story is like most others, with its various highs and

lows, successes and failures. It begins in 1976 on the night that I was born. The midwife who delivered me in the hospital was said to have had a strange look on her face when I entered the world. My mother asked her what was wrong but was assured that all was fine and there was no need for concern. Being a midwife herself, my mother knew that this woman had seen something unusual and she was determined to find out what it was. A few days later she caught up with the midwife and asked her, 'What was it you saw?'

'He had no innocence in his eyes, like he has seen it all before …' she replied.

Now, all these years later, I understand exactly what the midwife meant. I have always felt like I've been here before; this feeling is like a subconscious internal knowledge, a background murmur of familiarity. The story of the midwife was to provide me with the first of many clues that have helped me join the dots in my life and realise who I really am.

Dots to be Joined

As a child, I hated school. I felt trapped by it. The one activity I really loved was sailing. It offered me an escape from the pressures of life, and over the years I have been lucky enough to represent Ireland at several world and European championships. When I wasn't sailing, I was at my happiest exploring rock pools by the sea and fishing rather than playing with my peers. Yet those who know me well would say that I am extremely sociable. In many ways this has been a pattern throughout my life: the interweaving of black and white, contrasts and contradictions. As a Gemini perhaps it is to be expected.

During my time alone I pondered the world and why it is the way it is. It didn't make much sense to me; so many things lacked any order or reason. I couldn't understand the motivation behind people being mean or intolerant towards one another. It was beyond my comprehension. This meant that I started out as a quiet, serious, thoughtful child. It was only later that I rebelled against this philosophical view and evolved into a challenge seeker and adventurer.

The death of my Granddad, Andy O'Neill, in 1995 was a major turning point for me. His passing left a big hole in my life. On the surface I appeared fine. I had obviously developed my acting skills. But deep down I simply couldn't understand why he had been taken away. Granddad had been an amazing light in my life. An insurance salesman all his life, he always had a smile and a story for everyone he met. It was his sister who first introduced him to the Charismatic Healing Movement and he was instantly hooked. The Charismatic Renewal, as it is called, is a movement within the Catholic Church. It focuses on the gifts of the Holy Spirit, which are tongues: singing or chanting in a spontaneous language; prophecy: divine messages or insight; scripture: understanding and reading of the Bible; and last but not least, healing: the ability to cure ailments. Before long he had become a well-known healer and was conducting nightly sessions over the phone. Thousands of people either rang him or came to meet him for these healing sessions. As a child, little did I think that my Granddad's talents would be passed on to me. Today, through my healing work, I often sense his influence and feel the warmth of his smile.

College marked the next big chapter in my life and it was there that I met my wife Sarah. Our connection was instantaneous – she saw me and I saw her. By this I mean that our spirits recognised one another and saw beyond the masks that people in their twenties so often wear. Fourteen years later I am very lucky to still have Sarah and our beautiful son in my life. I realised just how important Sarah is to me when I was involved in a car crash some years ago. When I woke up she was the person I most wanted to see. I view that car crash as yet another major event – the joining of another dot – that has brought me one step closer to understanding life.

The crash happened after I had been attending a training session in Cork for a sailing world championship. My friend Max and I travelled back to his house in Wicklow. His father offered to give us a lift to Dublin. We were on the road only five minutes when two cars came hurtling towards us from the opposite side of the motorway. We collided head-on. I was in shock when I came around and my ears were ringing. I was reluctant to look behind me at the back seat for fear of the carnage I might see. Luckily, no one in our car had been badly injured. Of the passengers in the cars that hit us, two died and one fell into a coma. I firmly believe that a greater power saved me that day. I was in the front passenger seat and could easily have been killed. This incident was a wake-up call for me and from that day forth I began seizing every opportunity available to express myself and broaden my knowledge. I sometimes looked for opportunities in the wrong places so in many ways these years served to show me more about what I didn't want in life than what I did. However, I was in need of another dot. It presented itself some years later ...

Sarah and I got engaged and were to be married in April 2005. Then, three weeks before our wedding day, tragedy struck. While reading the Gospel in our local Catholic Church, my father had a major accident. The lectern at which he was standing was top-heavy and when he applied a small amount of his weight to it, it toppled over. He tried to grab a hold of it to steady himself but lost his balance and hit his head on the marble steps of the altar. My father suffered terrible head wounds and was given the last rites on the altar. An ambulance rushed him to hospital but he lapsed into a coma shortly after arrival. However, following a series of operations he regained consciousness. On the morning of our wedding he was disappointed he could not attend but was in good spirits. His advice to me was, 'keep going while the going is good'. I took this to mean, make the most of your life. Little did I know at the time that he wouldn't be with us for much longer. A few days into our honeymoon we got the call we'd been dreading; Dad had taken a turn. He passed away three weeks after we came home. This was a very surreal time in my life and many weighty questions began to take shape in my mind, not least of which was why, in the service of religion and God, had my father been taken away? I found myself re-evaluating my relationship with God, religion and spirituality.

AWAKENING THE MASCULINE FORCE

Following my father's passing, the next major milestone in my life was a four-day workshop in the UK run by US personal development guru Tony Robbins. I travelled to the workshop with work colleagues from the advertising agency I was working with at the time. The workshop included goal-setting, fire-walking, visualisation and work to remove mental barriers. Tony Robbins is the personification of yang (masculine) energy: strong, dynamic, forceful and driven. His message resonated with me because these were traits I recognised in myself. His workshop gave me four days to do something I had never done before – examine my life. I had what I like to call my first epiphany, or my yang (masculine) awakening, during this time. In the middle of a guided power visualisation I saw a crystal-clear image of what I wanted from my life: I saw myself helping people around the world to find their true selves. This image was powered by memories from my teens that proved to me I could make a difference. I taught sailing from the age of fourteen to twenty (and still do some coaching). I realised my greatest joy in giving these lessons was seeing my students' confidence blossom. I loved to see them walking taller and feeling better about themselves. At the same time I realised that what Tony Robbins was doing with the audience, in helping them to develop personally, was something that I could do. I was inspired by him.

Combining these realisations with my communication skills that had been honed through my marketing degree, advertising post-graduate course and years spent in the marketing and advertising business, my path became clear. I felt the call to teach and communicate during this epiphany, to help others realise their potential. In the healing business there is a term called 'clearing' which refers to the release of all the negative energy that you carry, be it emotionally, mentally, physically or spiritually. Well I must have cleared the previous thirty years of my life. Having always been very positive, I suddenly felt like I was on a rollercoaster, high one minute and low the next. I saw this as evidence that I was changing. I was like a butterfly shaking off a heavy cocoon. I felt a huge drive to help others. I then did one of the scariest things I have ever done in my life. I resigned from a very good job and set up Seachange Training, a company specialising in one-to-one coaching and the development of leadership and teambuilding in workplaces. Seachange has since allowed me to develop my motivational and communication skills.

DISCOVERING THE FEMALE FORCE

My second epiphany and my yin (feminine) awakening took place when, on the recommendation of a close friend called Ian Kingston, I visited the renowned Reiki healer Maria Rawlins. Maria gave me a Reiki treatment and described my energy and what was happening around me. No one had ever described me so accurately before. I found it liberating to know that someone else understood me. She told me about my feminine energy and that it was out of balance with my overarching masculine desire for success. I had never heard personal energy described in this way. She described in such a clear way how the feminine was the earth, explaining that the earth was like our mother, nurturing and nourishing us, but that we were not looking after her. Our neglect of the earth was like the neglect of our own feminine energy, in that we no longer trusted our intuition and had lost touch with our spirits. Most interestingly, she felt that my life's purpose was to lead people in a new way and to enlighten them about the energy of the feminine. This resonated very strongly with me and echoed my experience in Tony Robbins' workshop in the UK, except this time it was from a yin (feminine) perspective.

In the years that followed while I continued to run Seachange and help companies with their management issues and styles, I began learning about the healing arts of the ancient world. I studied Reiki and Seichem and qualified as a master and teacher in these areas some years later. During Reiki you are initiated into the way of the energy which is passed down from teacher to pupil all the way through the ages. Reiki comes from the Japanese words Rei meaning 'way' and Ki meaning 'energy' or 'life-force', thus meaning 'the way of energy'. It works on the principle that universal energy or Ki (chi) is everywhere. When we are out of balance the Ki in our systems is depleted and we then suffer sickness and disease either mentally, emotionally or physically. Reiki is the ancient art of balancing energy and the Reiki practitioner also acts as a conduit or channel to help this universal energy go to the recipient. It is the recipient that pulls in the energy while the practitioner simply facilitates the healing. Universal energy or life-force can be broken down into four elemental energies: fire, water, air and earth. Reiki is most closely linked with the element of earth. Seichem combines all four energies plus the energy of spirit, or 'Ether' as it is sometimes called by the ancients, and is what might be described as higher vibration or stronger energy than the more gentle Reiki energy.

Reiki transported me to a place of great peace and balance. I began to look more closely at the people around me, in particular at their sense of balance and peace. I realised that my spiritual journey had enabled me to empathise more easily with people. I became very aware of what was happening internally with my clients and others around me. I became equally perceptive in other areas, such as the environment, religion and society in general. Everywhere I looked I saw a massive imbalance of masculine and feminine energies, yet hardly anyone around me seemed aware of it. I felt a little like Galileo must have when he discovered the earth was round while everyone else still believed it to be flat. I needed to find a way to communicate this concept of balance. In my one-to-one coaching and business sessions I began using the language of masculine and feminine energies to explain the imbalance causing problems for the individual or the business. They understood it instantly. They were suddenly able to make sense of the world around them by looking at it through the vignette of yin (feminine) and yang (masculine). I knew I was on to something big, so I decided to write this book as a thought-provoking and practical tool to help others understand and balance their yin and yang energies.

READING GUIDE

Explore yourself

Thank you for deciding to read this book. In doing so, you have committed to delve deep into your mind to gain a new perspective on your life, your relationships, your career and your place in the world. The next few chapters will present you with a lot of new information and concepts and I urge you to continually ask yourself the question, 'Does this resonate with me?' In doing so, you will open up new and exciting channels of personal insight that will challenge many of your old belief systems.

You may be unfamiliar with the terms masculine and feminine in the context of energy. What we are exploring is not the differences between the sexes, but rather how these two primary universal energies affect our lives and the levels of success and happiness that we experience. As you will discover, men and women possess a combination of both masculine and feminine energies, as does nature, the world of business, etc. Throughout this book I will refer to the male energy as yang and the female energy as yin, as these terms readily embody the concept of these two great forces. The Chinese Tao scholars have used the terms for thousands of years. The Chinese used these two energies of masculine (yang) and feminine (yin) to explain the duality of the world. For example night and day, in and out, cold and heat, are all yin and yang respectively. As you will see, this vignette is really useful in helping us to understand the balance in the world and the relationship of the internal, personal, yin world, with the external, collective, yang world. I have found them a beautiful metaphor and template in which to unearth fascinating insights.

You may already be familiar with the yin yang symbol which acts as a visual metaphor for the nature and inter-dependence of the two forces:

Yin   =   Feminine energy (dark/black)
Yang =   Masculine energy (light/white)

So on reading something that surprises or interests you, stop and use your yang energy – your mind. Ask yourself, 'What do I *think* about this?' Then engage your yin energy in the form of your feelings or 'gut' and ask yourself, 'How do I *feel* about this?' In other words, put both your mental and your emotional abilities to work. In doing so you will quickly find that the two sometimes differ and sometimes agree. If you use only one facet of your perception – either just your mind or your gut – then you will only ever see half of the picture.

The thinking or yang response should come easy to us in the western world, while those in the eastern world will find the feeling or yin response easier. This is because by-in-large in the western world we have evolved to be very left brained or logical, which is to say yang-minded, while in the eastern world, where intuition and spirituality are stronger, people can interpret more readily that which the right mind struggles to fully understand, such as matters of a spiritual nature. Since most of you reading this book will be based in the western world, here is a simple method of engaging the yin or feeling mind. Place your hand on your gut, close your eyes and ask, 'What do I feel about this information?' Your gut feeling and intuition will tell you the answer. I realise that for many of you this approach will be a major departure from the norm. Please stick with it. You will quickly discover a new level of awareness and interpretation developing within you.

I hope that you enjoy this book and that it raises as many questions for you as it answers. Let this be the first step on a journey of both discovery of the self and of the world around you. For those of you who have already travelled many miles along your journey, I hope this book renews your passion for learning and growth by offering some insight into the dynamic force of the yin yang complex. I wish you an interesting and intriguing read.

When we see beyond what is the horizon of our knowledge and expose ourselves to new things, we can never again return to a place of unknowing, instead we are propelled forward in an everlasting quest to see what is beyond the horizon.

Chapter 1

The Yin Yang Complex

THE START OF THE JOURNEY

I can clearly recall the moment when it first struck me that the entire world is made up of masculine and feminine energies. I had just started secondary school and was attending my very first French class. The teacher was going over the fact that all nouns – people, places and things – are either masculine, feminine or neutral. I found this fascinating. How could a teapot be feminine? How could a knife be masculine? I was amazed that there was a language that described all of these items in such a manner. I was even more enthralled when the teacher called out a list of items and asked the class to guess whether they were masculine or feminine. Amazingly, most of us guessed correctly even though we had never spoken the language before. Looking back, I understand that on some level we sensed that things had either a masculine or a feminine energy – it was just that prior to this our young minds had

24

never considered this possibility. Or rather, somewhat closer to the truth, our society in general does not view the world in such terms. Yet somewhere inside us we instinctively knew the answers. Of course, for centuries many languages all over the world have classified things using masculine or feminine vocabulary. Many languages identify gender through the definite article or the ending of a word. The ancient language Alamblak, a tongue spoken in Papua New Guinea, has a fascinating way of categorising male or female energies. Anything that is long, tall or narrow is considered masculine. So snakes, spears, tall trees, roads, rivers and knives are all masculine. Whereas all things round, squat or wide are considered feminine, e.g. pots, bushes, houses, turtles and so on. Since the English language obviously does not assign nouns a gender in this way, it may give us a clue as to why the awareness of masculine and feminine energies is so low in countries where this is the main language.

Masculine and feminine energies are probably two of the oldest and most fundamental forces to have influenced the human dynamic. Our ancestors, the cavemen, learned from nature and the world around them. They saw themselves reflected in the rules of nature and in the universal connection of all things and beings. They believed that the masculine role was to hunt while the feminine role was to nurture. Their tribes developed along this principle and there was a very good reason for this. If a sabre-toothed tiger was lurking outside your cave you needed people in your tribe to focus on hurling rocks and spears to drive the danger away. Therefore, the masculine (yang) energy evolved to be about singular focus on a task. While Mr Ug was busy driving away sabre-toothed tigers, Mrs Ug was equally busy, but in a different way; she was multi-tasking – teaching, cooking and raising the children. It made evolutionary sense for the duties to be divided in this way. The combination of such diverse skills was key to the survival of our species. What has changed is that men and women now have a choice as to their roles and responsibilities in the home or in life. However, the same basic instincts that drove the cavemen/women still drive archetypal masculine and feminine approaches. This, as we will see, manifests itself in all aspects of our lives, both consciously and unconsciously.

All individuals contain a combination of both masculine and feminine energies. But some people are born with an excess of one or the other, giving rise to extreme characteristics such as aggression or over-sensitivity. If you think that I am referring to men firstly and women secondly, you would be mistaken. Men and women can fit either description. How many women do we see in high-powered careers who feel that the only way to succeed is by being tougher and more aggressive than men? These women often hide their feminine qualities of intuition, tact and emotional intelligence to compete with men. On the other hand, we have the over-sensitive man who tries too hard to please everyone, adopting a feminine perspective to the detriment of his perception as a man. He has become so sensitive that all his drive and ambition have been lost. Both these descriptions may seem extreme, but they are more common than you might think. Most of us primarily contain the energy of our sex. So a man will be mostly masculine in his approach, or yang as the Chinese would say, while a woman will be mostly feminine, owing to what are called yin characteristics. People are generally a combination of the two energies: men being maybe 75 per cent masculine energy and 25 per cent feminine energy, while women are the opposite. Some people can oscillate, moving from a feminine energy approach to a masculine approach depending on the circumstances.

So what traits make up these two energies? Yin, the feminine energy, is creative, intuitive, flowing, harmonious, nurturing, inward-drawing, reflective, containing, considerate, qualitative and loving. All of these traits belong in the positive realm. Negative feminine energy manifests as manipulation, underhandedness, jealousy, bitterness and discord. On a physical level the feminine is the left-hand side of the body and the right hemisphere of the brain. (Each side of the body is controlled by the opposite side of the brain.) The feminine is also your emotional intelligence and your spiritual energy. As a symbol it can most easily be described as a circle or sphere or, if you like, the womb.

In the case of yang, or the masculine energy, the forces

at work are strength, action, forcefulness, goal orientation, productivity, exuberance, dynamism, adventurousness, innovation, outward moving. Again these are the positives. In its negative realm we see war, oppression and tyranny. In the physical state the masculine is the right-hand side of the body and the left hemisphere of the brain. The yang is your mind or IQ and your physical body. As a symbol, it is represented by a line or a cylinder, in other words a phallic symbol.

YOUR MASCULINE AND FEMININE ENERGIES

Masculine Energy (yang)	*Feminine Energy (yin)*
Positive Forces Strength, activeness, thinking, forcefulness, goal orientation, productiveness, quantitative-orientation, exuberance, dynamism, adventurousness, innovation, outward moving, structured, achievement-orientation, extravert, judging	**Positive Forces** Creative, intuitive, flowing, beginnings and ends, harmonious, nurturing, inward drawing, reflective, containing, considerate, qualitative-orientation, loving, introverted, feeling, perceptive, knowing
Negative Forces War, oppression, corruption and tyranny	**Negative Forces** Manipulation, underhandedness, bitterness
Physical Body The right-hand side of the body and the left hemisphere of the brain	**Physical Body** The left-hand side of the body and the right hemisphere of the brain

Elements Fire and air	**Elements** earth and water
Colours Red, yellow, gold and brightness	**Colours** Green, blue, silver and darkness
Planets Sun, Mars, Uranus and Jupiter	**Planets** Moon, Venus, Saturn, Neptune and Pluto
Movement Outward, ascending and vertical	**Movement** Inward, descending and horizontal
Essence The mental self and the physical self	**Essence** The emotional self and the spiritual self
Intelligence Intelligence Quotient (IQ)	**Intelligence** Emotional Intelligence (EI)
Archetypes The king, the father, the warrior, the wizard, the son, the youth, the villain, the prince, the priest, the philosopher, the shaman, the sailor, the hero, the hermit, the god, the grandfather Both sexes – the joker/fool/angel/fairy	**Archetypes** The queen, the mother, the virgin, the crone, the witch, the temptress, the siren, the bride, the wife, the daughter, the princess, the priestess, the heroine, the goddess, the grandmother Both sexes – the joker/fool/angel/fairy

The lack of awareness of the feminine and masculine principle is more of a western affliction than a global one, due to the dark age that Europe suffered and the repression of herbalists, folk medicine and healers by the Catholic Church, who considered them heretics and witches. Bodies of knowledge in the East like traditional Chinese medicine and the Ayurvedic medicine of India stretch back 2,000 and 5,000 years respectively. Compare this to western medicine, which is about 300 years old and you get a good indication of the depth and ancientness of eastern knowledge.

Lack of balance is a relatively modern problem. Drawings on cave walls dating from the Palaeolithic period (35000–9000 BC) show the feminine being worshipped as the cradle of life and the masculine as the hunter. Both were equal, with each sex occupying and embodying key energies and roles, and both were two sides of the same coin, different but cast at the same time and both requiring the other to function. To understand these people we cannot think in terms of the gender equality of today. Quite simply they realised that nature needed both masculine and feminine energy to function and they could see that they were simply reflections of this. The fact that they painted warriors hunting and women with big breasts and hips may also suggest that they revered these things and recognised them as being significant in life. Almost all ancient peoples believed in this duality. The Chinese Tao, one of the oldest schools of thought in China, believed the world could be explained in terms of the yin and the yang. Together, the masculine and feminine energies achieve perfect equilibrium. The yin yang symbol shows the fluid and harmonious relationship between the two forces. While both yin and yang are 90 per cent pure, they contain 10 per cent of the other.

This balance of male and female is also very evident in Native American Indian culture where the earth is called 'Mother earth' and the sky 'Father Sky'. The Indians were not alone. The ancient Greeks also believed in father sky, who they called Zeus, and mother earth who they called Demeter. The Celts, the Aztecs, the Mayans, the Egyptians and the Tibetans all have circular mandalas and other symbols denoting the balance between the male and female energies. Hippocrates, whose oath all medical professionals swear, compared man to the elements of fire and air – red and yellow – and women to earth and water – green and blue.[1] It is more than just a coincidence that all of these ancient religions and belief systems offer the same concept of masculine and feminine energies, especially seeing as many of these civilisations had little or no contact with one another. Yet in the modern-day western world we have scarcely any awareness of the incredible and dynamic energies that surround us.

The main question for all of us in terms of our personal development is how do these energies manifest in us? Are you a kind, considerate and loving woman who lacks the drive and energy required to achieve certain goals in your life? Are you a competitive, career-driven, goal-focused man who struggles to relate to your partner, children and others around you? All of us have strengths and weaknesses that stem from our individual balance of masculine and feminine energies. If you fail to effectively balance the yin and yang energies within you, then you will fail to lead a fulfilled and happy existence.

The cost of this imbalance is high. It can manifest on a physical level as sickness and disease, on an emotional level as turmoil, anger or depression, on a mental level as stress and panic, or on a spiritual level as a sense of emptiness and disconnection. I am not suggesting that finding a balance between your yin and yang is a panacea for all ills, but rather that by combining the collective wisdom of the ages with the power of modern science you will discover a remedy, framework or vignette through which to view and understand the complex world we live in. I believe that using this concept will help you to take responsibility for your well-being and to regain control of your levels of happiness and fulfilment. Luckily, achieving this balance is easier than you might think. There are three fundamental steps involved in balancing your yin and yang forces:

Step 1: Become aware of your balance of masculine and feminine energy.

Step 2: Identify which areas of your yin or yang need strengthening and on what level: mental, emotional, physical or spiritual.

Step 3: Live everyday in balance to achieve maximum happiness and success.

Throughout this book I will guide you in how to achieve this awareness, how to identify which levels you require balance on and how to live in balance to ensure the happiness you deserve. The following exercise will help you to connect with your body, your mind and your yin and yang.

EXERCISE

Guided Relaxation – Meet your yin and yang

This guided relaxation will help you get in touch with your masculine and feminine energies. You can record this passage and re-play it to yourself or get your partner or a friend to read it aloud to you. Alternatively, you can purchase *The Yin Yang Complex* CD from www.brendanfoley.ie. You may also simply visualise this meditation as you read.

To begin, make sure you are seated comfortably. Remove your shoes and take the phone off the hook so that you won't be interrupted. Make the space you use special. If you have a scented candle or some incense, please use them to set the mood.

Sit comfortably with your feet flat on the ground. Feel the support of the chair against your back. Rest your palms on your thighs. Close your eyes and become aware of your breathing.

Take five deep breaths. Let each breath go down to your belly button. When you exhale feel all the stale air in your lungs being expelled. One, breathing deeply, allow your lungs to fill … hold for three seconds … and exhale. Two, breathing deeply, feel your lungs fill with air and hold for three seconds. Exhale deeply. Three, feel yourself relax as you breathe deeply and hold for three seconds, exhale deeply. Four, feeling great as you inhale, hold for three seconds and exhale. Five, take a final deep breath, hold and exhale. Now allow your breathing to settle at a natural pace.

Very slowly become aware of the sensation of your body. Feel the ground beneath your feet. Feel your palms resting on your thighs, feel your back supported by the chair. Become aware of the sounds around you. What is the furthest-away sound you can hear? Become aware of it and let it go. Now move inward. What is the next closest sound you can hear? Again, become aware of it and let it go. Once more, what sound is next closest? Become aware of it and let it go. Keep repeating this process until you are listening to the sound of your own breathing. You may even be able to hear the sound of your own heartbeat.

Notice how your body has relaxed. Now become aware of the warmth of your breath as you breathe out and the coolness as you breathe in. Focus on this, allowing yourself to relax with each breath you take, nice and easy, feeling all the stress and tension leave your body with each breath. Keep breathing, keep relaxing, keep letting go.

Become aware of a beautiful light above your head. This light can be any colour you want. See, sense, feel or imagine this beautiful light. Feel or see how it shines. Feel its temperature. Very slowly this light starts to descend. You feel it touch your scalp. Feel how the muscles of your scalp relax. Feel the light come down into your head, filling your mind. Feel the light behind your eyes. All the muscles in your brow and your eyes relax. Feel all tension and strain leave your body.

The light continues down into your neck. Feel all the stress and tension stored here dissipate. You feel your jaw and your tongue relax and the walls of your throat soften, all the time breathing softly and easily, becoming more and more relaxed. Feel the light continue down into your chest and shoulders. Feel it travel down your left arm, relaxing as it goes. You feel your shoulder, elbow and wrist become soft, all tension leaving the joints. Feel the light do the same with your right arm, releasing, relaxing, letting go. The light fills your lungs and you feel it go into your blood and radiate around your body. Feel the light bathing your whole back. Feel all the stress and strain leave your body. Feel your abdomen fill fully with this beautiful light, all the time becoming more and more relaxed.

The light moves down through your hips, relaxing them as it goes, and slowly flows down your left leg, relaxing the knee, ankle and foot. Feel the light flow down your right leg, easing as it goes. Letting go. Feel your right knee, ankle and foot relax. You are now completely bathed in a brilliant, beautiful, healing and relaxing light. In this state you will be able to access both your masculine and feminine energies.

Say to yourself, 'I am my masculine energy. I am my male energy. I am the masculine energy of —— saying your name at this point. Again say, 'I am my masculine energy.'

Ask your higher self, your subconscious, your spirit or whatever you feel to be your inner self to make you fully aware of your masculine energy. Breathe and allow your masculine energy to flow. That's right, let go, surrender to this energy that is inside you. Feel how strong it is. What does it feel like? Where do you feel it? Can you feel it in your physical body? How does it feel in your mind? Let the sensations grow, keep letting go and you will experience more of your yang side, your masculine side. What colour is this masculine energy? What does it feel like? Breathe it in. Feel it wash over you. Feel the intensity of it. If your masculine energy could talk what would it say to you? Would it have a message for you? Would it request you do something? Just relax in your masculine energy for a moment.

Now it is time to let go of this energy. Let it slip away. Feel the energy go back to its normal level. Feel it flow away and back to where it came from. Feel yourself become more centred as the strong yang energy relaxes and you return to a gentle resting state. Let it all go so that you can now embrace and invoke your feminine energy – your yin side.

Now say to yourself, 'I am my feminine energy. I am the feminine energy of ——' and say your name. Say, 'I am my yin side. I am the female energy. I am my feminine side.' Ask your inner self, your higher self or your spirit to allow you to feel the full extent of your feminine energy. Feel its subtle expansive nature as it rolls in, feel yourself immersed in the yin. Feel your feminine energy rise to the top. Immerse yourself in it. Allow it to grow stronger and stronger. Allow yourself to fully let go, to fully experience this feminine energy. Where do you feel it in your body? Where is it centred? What colour is it? What do you sense? Now allow yourself to go even deeper into it. Feel how it consumes you. If your feminine energy could talk to you what would it say? What message would it give you? Now, go even deeper. What messages are you getting? It may be words, sounds or imagery, or come to you as a feeling or a sense. Breathe it in.

Allow yourself to relax in your yin side. Feel and explore it. Allow it to guide you. Take a moment just to soak it all in.

Now, listen to your breathing and let your yin side slip away, knowing that once you have accessed this side of yourself, you can come back any time you wish. This is a special place inside of you. You have now experienced the wonder of the male and female energies that drive your character and shape your world. Feel the two energies or visualise them blending into one, into a complete and balanced energy. You will be able to use this new balance to assist you in further exploring your character.

Very slowly become aware of the room you are in. Allow your body and mind to return to a full state of awakening. Five, take a deep breath and allow your body to be filled with air. Four, another deep breath and this time wiggle your fingers and toes. Three, breathe deeply again and stretch your arms and legs. Two, another deep breath, feeling fully energised and renewed. One, fully awake.

Well done. Take a moment to ground yourself and make sure to drink plenty of water following this exercise in relaxation.

Chapter 2

Recognising Your Yin and Yang Sides

MEET YOUR YIN AND YANG

'The brighter the light, the darker the shadow,' the psychotherapy pioneer Carl Jung once remarked. This comment says a lot about the dichotomy that exists within us. We are a conundrum of masculine and feminine energies, some positive, some negative. It is only by understanding these forces that shape us that we can come to a place of full personal awareness – a place of enlightenment.

To be successful, happy and fulfilled you need to understand yourself. For to know thyself is to know the world. This piece of ancient wisdom can also be summed up in the beautiful sayings, 'As within, so without', or 'As above, so below'. They refer to the fact that our external world is simply a reflection of our internal world, with our perception of reality determining our reality. How we interpret the world around us affects our thoughts and emotions. Most people will have experienced a sense of their perception of a situation differing from the reality of it. How many times have you been overcome by dread at the thought of doing something – whether it was learning a new skill, saying sorry to someone or pursuing a goal? We frequently find ourselves paralysed by a fear that we have created in our own heads and has no basis in reality. It is not a rational fear but an overblown assessment of what would happen should we fail. However, if you succeed in conquering this fear you can turn what was once a weakness into a strength. Conquering fear creates confidence and builds up our ability to succeed in the world. The lesson for us here is to 'feel the fear and do it anyway', as Susan Jeffers writes in her great book of the same title.

In this chapter I will challenge you to really explore your personality. There is no need to fear what you might find as we all possess a mixture of brightness and darkness. It is only by accepting and understanding the forces at work inside us that we can truly start to grow and, more importantly, understand ourselves, others and the world around us. Having looked at the masculine and feminine energies chart in Chapter 1, you will already have identified some of your own traits. These energies are most simply expressed as ego and empathy – ego being the masculine trait, the yang, and empathy being the feminine trait, the yin. It is worth dwelling on the nature of each trait for a moment to gain a greater understanding of these two forces.

Ego is about power, a sense of pride, control and dominance. The ego as described by the *Merriam-Webster Dictionary* is 'the self especially as contrasted with another self or world'. It is bound by itself and its own achievements and desires. It works only to further itself. The word ego derives from Latin and means self. The masculine energy can clearly be seen as the ego's drive to succeed and control in the interest of the self. This is not a bad thing if it is balanced by empathy, or the feminine. The word empathy derives from the Greek word *pathos* which means feeling. It is about understanding outside of the self, in particular other people. This is the feminine principle. The *Merriam-Webster Dictionary* defines empathy as 'the action of understanding, being aware of, being sensitive to, and vicariously experiencing the feelings, thoughts, and experience of another of either the past or present without having the feelings, thoughts, and experience fully communicated in an objectively explicit manner'. Empathy comes into play when we talk about 'putting ourselves in someone else's shoes'. We often make this remark when we are trying to imagine how someone else feels about a situation. Nelson Mandela provided one of the most beautiful examples of empathy during his inauguration as president of South Africa when he applauded the security forces that had kept him in prison for over twenty-eight years:

We would also like to pay tribute to our security forces, in all their ranks, for the distinguished role they have played in securing our first democratic elections and the transition to democracy from blood-thirsty forces which still refuse to see the light. The time for the healing of the wounds has come. The moment to bridge the chasms that divide us has come. The time to build is upon us.

Here is someone who was able to stand in the shoes of his oppressors and thereby find it in his heart to work with them.

While the ego represents the yang drive to personally succeed, empathy represents the yin drive to find balance and reach out to others. Together, the two energies form a powerful alliance of horizontal and vertical consciousness that delivers equilibrium. Horizontal consciousness consists of thoughts and feelings that move outward and encompass a great range and breath. Vertical consciousness, on the other hand, comprises thoughts and feelings that focus on deepening and directing our energy in a very specific way. Remove the yang and we get a situation that is caring, empathetic and inclusive but lacking the driving energy to create any action. Remove the yin and we get a situation where personal gain, action and power take precedence over other people and, ironically, given time, the self. Both yin and yang need to be balanced inside of us. As we continue to explore these two primary energies we will see that they can be subdivided and applied to the four main aspects of character: mind, body, spirit and emotion.

So where on the ego/empathy scale do you sit? Are you self-obsessed and determined to pursue the goals and desires of your ego to the detriment of those around you? Or are you the opposite? The humanitarian dedicated to understanding and improving the lives of others and neglecting your own needs in the process. Or are you both? In the western world most of us are the former rather than the latter. We are the product of a society that places the ego at the very heart of its concept of success. Yet on some level all of us want to be more caring, open and understanding. We all need a mix of both ego and empathy, masculine and feminine, yin and yang. To be all of one type of energy would mean a state of total imbalance. If you want to save the world you will need to begin by working on your feminine sense of empathy and balance; this will motivate you to want to pursue your cause. This then needs to be coupled with the masculine ability to take action. So to summarise, your yin makes you aware of the injustice around you while your yang enables you to do something about it. We need to develop a balance. As I will explore in later chapters, history has endowed most of us with a yang legacy. So you could say that the bedrock or base programming of western society is yang or under the masculine influence.

ARCHETYPES

An archetype is an innate prototype or pattern found within a personality trait. It is thought that Plato first used the term which, when translated from ancient Greek, literally means 'first moulded'. This suggests an ancient pattern of energy that has been present in mankind since the beginning. Down through the ages, from the Greek legends to the works of Shakespeare to modern-day cinema and theatre, we can see archetypes being played out. They are bundles of energy that seem to reappear time and time again throughout the human story in the form of the hero, the warrior, the lover and so on. Some of these archetypes are positive, such as the mother, while others are negative, such as the victim. Some are masculine in nature and therefore yang, others are feminine in nature and therefore yin.

Earlier, I mentioned Carl Jung, one of the founding fathers of psychotherapy. Jung looked at archetypes within Greek myths, the Egyptian culture and the Tarot cards, and compiled what is referred to in psychology as the Jungian archetypes. If you have ever completed a personality assessment or a work-style profile for your career then you have probably come into contact with Jung without even realising it. The modern analysis of personality types was the brainchild of Jung. The most widely known of these tests is the Myers Briggs Type Indicator (MBTI) which is based indirectly on Jung's work. It works on the premise that people can be analysed using four scales:

1) Thinking or feeling
2) Sensing or intuition
3) Introversion or extraversion
4) Perceiving or judging

The masculine traits of yang are thinking, sensitive, extraverted and judging. The yin traits are feeling, intuition, introverted and perceiving. It is quite clear why thinking and feeling are yang and yin. The thinking brain is powered by the masculine impetus while feeling is driven by the feminine power. Sensing and intuition, on the other hand, prove more complex. Sensing in this instance is masculine as it is a reactive quality based on external stimuli, while intuition is feminine as it is based on internal gut feelings and creative insight. Extraversion is very yang as it relies on external motivation from others, while introversion is yin as it is internally motivated. Perception is yin – it is about seeing the whole picture, unhindered by the ego, and without needing to take action on what you see. Judging is a masculine trait. It requires that a decision be taken on whether the subject matter at hand is good, bad or indifferent, after which action must be taken to either support the good or oppose the bad. If we look at the dichotomies of the MBTI we can see a clear division.

Dichotomies of the Myers Briggs Type Indicator (MBTI)	
Feminine Energy (yin)	Masculine Energy (yang)
Introversion	Extraversion
Intuition	Sensing
Feeling	Thinking
Perceiving	Judging

There are many online tests that you can take to see where you rank on the MBTI scale. If you do a search for 'Jung Test' or 'MBTI Test' you will find a number of tests that will yield a four-letter result. My personal result reveals that I am an ENFP. This means I am inclined towards being extraverted, intuitive, feeling and perceptive. What I find most interesting about this result is what it says about the balance of my masculine and feminine energies. It indicates that I have a masculine energy in the form of my extraversion, while intuition, feeling and perception make up my feminine energy. It is very important to understand that this is not an assessment of physical gender but rather an insight into the nature of the energy that shapes your thoughts, feelings, attitudes and beliefs. This mix of ENFP also provides a strong indication of the type of career or vocation a person might be attracted to. As a coach, teacher and communicator, my profile confirms my need to help and understand people and have an audience for my extraversion. My profile would not suggest a career as a financial trader or a military man. My MBTI result reassures me that my life energy is in keeping with my work. Many of you will find the same, while others will most certainly find that they are in the wrong profession. If you decide not to take the test, by looking at the 'Dichotomies' you can recognise your strongest traits. Choose at least one attribute from each line. Which side do you lean towards? What is your mix? Does your role or career reflect your balance?

Masculine and feminine energies are not just polarised according to the MBTI scale. There are many diverse masculine and feminine archetypes playing out all around us. In fact, our entertainment industry is largely based on these archetypes. Soap operas, films, plays, books, comics and computer games all make use of these well-known yin and yang archetypes: the villain, the hero, the heroine, the sage, the witch, the virgin, the joker and so on. We love seeing these characters enacted as they reflect aspects of our own selves – our dark side and our light, our masculine and our feminine. By engaging with these forms of entertainment we are in fact engaging with our archetypes. If you think of such great films as *Star Wars, Casablanca, The Lord of the Rings* or *The Shawshank Redemption* I'm sure you have a list of favourite characters because you recognise in them some of the archetypes that make up your own unique personality pattern. Perhaps you see yourself in the wise sage Yoda or the hero Luke Skywalker; or perhaps in the lover archetype of Princess Leia or the villainous Darth Vader. The character that most resonates with you provides a clue to your own archetypal traits. All archetypes can be divided into yin and yang, masculine and feminine.

The ancients understood that personality types come in bundles. Ptolemy, who is credited as the father of mathematics and philosophy, wrote extensively on archetypes. In fact, archetypes crop up time and time again in the ancient legends of every civilisation. Take the brave warrior prince Luke Skywalker in *Star Wars* for example: in Celtic lore he is Fionn Mac Cumhaill; in the Indian Vedic tradition he is Arjuna; and in the Greek legends he is Hector. We can see the sage shape-shifting wizard Merlin of English and Norse tradition in *The Matrix* in the character of Morpheus as played by Laurence Fishburne. Incidentally, the name Morpheus is taken from the Greek god of dreams. The most common feminine archetype is that of the Divine Mother. She is Demeter, the Greek mother earth, bringer of the seasons and the harvest; she is Kwan Yin, the Buddhist divine mother figure; she is Mother Mary, the Christian feminine archetype; she is Isis, the Egyptian goddess; and she is Lakshmi, the feminine balance to Krishna in the Hindu tradition. She can be loving one minute and life-ending the next. The feminine principle represents birth and death. She can be the bringer of life or can possess the powerful but potentially destructive energy of Boudicca or Joan of Arc. Some of the most powerful screen actresses, such as Brenda Fricker and Susan Sarandon, can be both mothering and loving but at the same time they are powerful energies who are admired and respected.

The joker, the fool or the trickster is another common character in legends. The trickster was recognised by Carl Jung as an archetype in his work on understanding human psychology.[2] The Native Americans' trickster comes in the form of the coyote and the raven. In Scandinavian legends the god Loki is known as the trickster; in the Greek legend Prometheus stole the spark of creativity from the gods. The joker, fool and trickster is essentially a creative archetype: in the case of Prometheus he stole the spark of creativity and in doing so could now think for himself and create fun and mischief. The fool card in the Tarot deck refers to the start of something new or the number 0, the place from where all things start or where the creative spark to do something new is found. All cultures have these archetypes, which are a mix of masculine and feminine energy portrayed in either their positive or negative manifestations. In the modern era, the trickster still generates the same levels of fascination. The trickster's tendency towards self-sabotage will resonate with most of us.

Think of your three favourite characters from TV or film. Are they mostly yin or yang? Are they positive or negative? What archetypal energy do they hold for you? Interestingly, in most cultures the joker archetype is seen as the dark side of both the masculine and feminine energies, and across the different legends it appears as both sexes. Creativity is key to comedians and jokers – it is their ability to deliver a message or recite something in a new and creative way that creates their success. Look at Jim Carrey, Eddie Izzard or any of the top comics – they shape-shift, changing character almost in front of our eyes. In the old mythology the trickster could change sex and shape, appearing in quick succession as a variety of characters. Many of today's comedians are brilliant impressionists, changing sex, voice, posture and costume to parody or give humorous impressions of those around them or public figures.

The fool archetype still exists today – just pick up any deck of playing cards and you'll find a joker in the pack. Incidentally, this provides us with a clue as to the origin of playing cards – they derive from the original tarot card deck. The original tarot contains all the archetypes and these cards were used during the Middle Ages to teach people about the different personality traits. The kings, queens and jokers were all present, as in your normal playing cards, but other archetypes were also included, such as the hermit, the emperor, the hanged man, the tower, the knight, the lovers, the magician and many more. The cards doubled as an oracle and as a source of education for a mostly illiterate population who could learn about life energies through the form of games.

All cultures have the various mixes of masculine and feminine energy portrayed in their positive or negative manifestations. These archetypes have always found expression through different forms of entertainment. In Elizabethan times, Shakespeare's plays enjoyed so much success largely due to his talent at breathing life into these archetypes. The actors in his plays were practically social outcasts as it was thought that they invoked spirit, the ancient energies of the gods, archetypes and those who had passed on before. As Paddy McCoey, the Irish theatre director, teacher and workshop facilitator says, 'they [the actors] were believed to be shape-shifters and beyond the Church ... When Macbeth was first performed, the audience actually believed that magic and sorcery was really taking place in front of them. You must remember that magic, mystery and all things connected to the other worlds was a potent force within the culture. Also fear played a huge role in the culture and thinking of the times, often used by the Church as a weapon of control. England had just freed itself from what it saw as the tyranny of Rome and was deep in the reformation initiated by Henry VIII and continued by his daughter Elizabeth I. It was also known as a golden age, when the spiritual/political/social landscape of Europe was shifting. Perhaps that is why Shakespeare was able to reach so deeply and comprehensively into the very souls of a nation.'[3] The theatre has always created a rich sense of the transcendental. In its essence, this is the feminine energy – the ability to empathise so fully with a character or archetype that you become the character, in the sense that you can live their emotion or physical sensation.

The pioneers in the area of archetypes – Freud, Jung and Adler – all believed that while society has a huge effect on how we develop, we are all born with a mixture of masculine and feminine energies. Jung identified these energies as the anima in men and the animus in women and he believed that both were unconscious aspects of character. The anima in men referred to their feminine side and contained an image of the woman as a mother, a lover or a crone. Jung believed that this aspect of a man's character enabled him to understand the opposite sex. The positive side of the anima manifests in men as intuition, an appreciation of nature and a love of the self, and serves as a guide to spiritual and emotional development. The more in touch a man is with his feminine side, the better he is at interacting with women. Jung proposed that the dark side of the feminine in the man manifests as dark moods of depression and insecurity. He added that the relationship men shared with their mothers brought out either the light or the dark side of their yin – a good relationship bringing out the light and vice-versa.

In women, Jung described the animus as the unconscious male archetype, containing images of the prince, the father and the sage. Again, the woman's relationship with her father was a huge influence, with a good one bringing out the light side of the masculine qualities, such as the will to act, decisiveness, judgment and discrimination. In its dark side, the animus reveals itself as the need to constantly argue and be proven right. Jung felt that to repress either the anima or animus would be to deny an essential component of the personality. The dark side of these archetypes would then come into play, eventually forcing the conscious mind to take notice and acknowledge their existence. In later chapters I will discuss the impact the inbuilt anima and animus have on who we are attracted to in life.

To create balance in our lives, we must first identify the archetypes being enacted on our own stage. One way of doing this is to examine the fourteen major archetypes as observed by the chakra system. The chakra system originated in India in around 3000 BC. The word chakra means 'wheel' or 'vortex' in Sanskrit, one of the official languages of India, and refers to energy centres located on various points of our bodies. The root chakra lies at the base of the spine and the energy centres move upwards from there in a line all the way to the crown of the head. Whether or not you subscribe to this belief system, it is nonetheless interesting to note the archetypes associated with each chakra.

The basic premise is that we all have seven chakras, each of which has a corresponding positive and negative archetype. These chakras also represent our greatest strengths and weaknesses. For example a problem or low energy in your root chakra may see you play the role of the victim, while a strong and healthy throat chakra will see you able to speak with authority. In her book *Chakras and their Archetypes*, Ambika Wauters describes the breakdown of these chakras as follows:[4]

Chakra	Negative Archetypes	Positive Archetypes
Root	Victim	Mother
Sacral	Martyr	Emperor/Empress
Solar	Servant	Warrior
Heart	Actor	Lover
Throat	Silent Child	Communicator
Brow	Intellectual	Intuitive
Crown	Egotist	Guru

Which of these archetypes resonates most strongly with you? What is your dark side? What is your light side? Remember that to some degree, independent of your gender, all of these archetypes reside within you. Those that are most dominant in our psychology tend to create the situations that cause us either great happiness or intense pain. All of the archetypes mentioned can manifest as either yin or yang. For example, the warrior may use persuasion and guile to fight for what is right, a yin energy, or use force and power to achieve his goal, these being yang traits.

Once you are aware of your internal forces, you must then decide on the best course of action to steer you towards the positive aspects of your nature. For example, if the egotist/guru opposition resonates with you, then you may find that you are respected for your opinions and tend to search for a greater good in the work you do. This is the upside – the guru.

The downside may be that you have impure motives; you may be secretly motivated by a desire for fame or a boost to your self-esteem. As you lean towards the side of the egotist, the advice you give to others may be tainted by your ego and your desire to be duly rewarded for your work. Your ability to advise is therefore compromised.

On the other hand, take the common scenario of the victim/mother opposition. The victim is convinced that the whole world is out to get them. They believe failure is their only companion and expect to meet it at every turn. They revel in this sense of being downtrodden to the point that victimhood becomes their identity. Some even seem proud of their lot, boasting about how bad their life is in comparison to everyone else. Their incessant complaints attract attention from their peers and they misinterpret this as love. They are caught in a vicious circle, forced to permanently revel in misfortune to ensure a constant flow of sympathy from those around them. Unfortunately, this eventually takes its toll on them mentally, emotionally, physically and spiritually, and reduces them to a truly miserable existence. Only by facing their demons and learning to love themselves can they activate the positive archetype of the mother. When the mother archetype is present, the person is able to love and nurture themselves, and teach and cherish their mental, emotional, physical and spiritual being. This base of self-love enables them to recognise true love in others and thereby admit this love into their lives.

Any negative archetypes you identify within yourself need to be acknowledged and balanced. The very act of being aware of them immediately deflates their effect. Your higher self identifies an impostor in your psychology and from that point on its negative impact can be seen and understood. This gives rise to the conditions necessary for change. The more you explore your archetypes, the more you will come to understand the balance of your yin and yang. Recognition is the key to creating change; it is the first step in transformation. Awareness creates the 'right view' or a true view of your psychology at a particular moment in time. 'Right view' and 'right action' are Buddhist concepts. Right view is the ability to see the truth of a situation in terms of how it relates to you, the people around you and anyone else that you affect in any way. Right view is yin in nature as it is inward-looking and demands observation rather than judgment. You can use the archetypes as a tool to help you acquire the right view. Once you are confident that you have become aware of who you are and are more familiar with your yin and yang energies, you will then need to implement the second part of the principle, right action. This is a yang energy as it is based on actualisation. Right action is about knowing the right thing to do and basing it on the knowledge you have acquired. Creating the right action in this context means bringing about a change in yourself that will balance your yin and yang. This, in turn, will increase both your own happiness, radiate to others and give you a sense of place and purpose.

Chapter 3

Creating a Personal
Yin Yang Balance

THE PATH TO BALANCE

By now you should have some inkling as to which of your energies you need to develop. Is your yin deficient? Or perhaps it is your yang? Which do you need to strengthen? Or maybe they both need strengthening. There are an infinite number of ways that you can begin to balance your yin and yang and each person will have different requirements. I will outline some of the most effective ways of strengthening your yin or yang, or both. These remedies fall under the four main aspects of being: mental, emotional, spiritual and physical. Please go through each exercise at the end of this chapter. The exercise that resonates strongly or intrigues you the most is probably the most important one for you to complete.

PHYSICAL BALANCING

Our physical bodies serve as an incredible barometer for our inner state of being. If we are stressed we all know that this can manifest in physical symptoms. These can include rashes, pains in the neck, back and shoulders, irritable bowels and tension in the stomach and intestines. There is an intrinsic link between our mental, spiritual, emotional and physical states. While this link can sometimes have negative consequences, the good news is that we can also direct this same principle towards positive ends. Our physical body can send messages to our emotional, spiritual and mental selves and induce balance in them. As early as 1906 the scientist Israel Waynbaum claimed that our facial expression can come before the attending emotion. In the 1960s Dr Robert Zajonc of the University of Michigan tested and proved Waynbaum's theory. In other words we can create our emotional state by choosing what we want it to be. Psychologist Paul Ekman at the University of California found similar results. By getting actors to put on the various emotions the human face can express, the researchers found that their subjects began to feel the emotion they were demonstrating.[5]

Continuing in this vein, we are now going to get your body to send balanced yin and yang messages to your whole being.

Firstly, let us identify whether your body is primarily yin or yang. All of us are a mixture of both but will usually lean more heavily on one side or the other. Look at the

chart below and tick the boxes that describe you most
accurately:

Yin Body	Yang Body
Sleep curled up	Sleep stretched out
Sleepiness	Insomnia
Pale face	Red face
Weak voice, silent	Strong voice, talkative
Pale tongue, white coat	Red tongue, yellow coat
Slight pulse	Strong pulse
Relaxed	Excitable
Tendency to feel cold	Tendency to feel hot
Energy tends towards listlessness	Energy tends towards hyperactivity
Slow moving	Fast moving
Tendency to retain water	Dehydrate easily
Carry extra fatty tissue	Thin
Broad short muscles	Long thin muscles
Large torso and broad legs and arms	Slim build
Total:	Total:

There are no right or wrong answers. The most important thing is to reveal if you have a physical tendency towards yin or yang. While some of you will be very balanced, others will lean towards extremes. If you believe you are not in balance, consider opting for traditional Chinese medicine (TCM) or Amatsu, a treatment based on body alignment. TCM draws heavily on this chart when diagnosing illness, incorporating the principle of balance – yin and yang will always seek to balance each other. TCM uses a process of oral medicine, acupuncture and heat treatment to help the body to balance, and works on the four levels of body, mind, emotion and spirit. Amatsu is a 5,000-year-old Japanese practice which focuses on balancing the physical body and in doing so balances mind, body, emotional and spirit. It is a physical therapy involving movement, massage and muscle testing. It has become popular with many osteopaths and chiropractors in the West over the last few years.[6]

The following is a simple physical-stimulus exercise that can be carried out in the morning time. It creates balance by sending signals around your body that activate energy meridians and acupuncture points. It works to achieve balance between the masculine and feminine energies in the body.

Balancing Exercise[7]

1. Rub the crown of your head (the top) and coccyx (the bottom or tail bone) simultaneously to energise your spine.

2. Left and right sides of the body – place your hands on opposite shoulders. Gently twist three times to the left and three times to the right. Repeat with hands on opposite hips and take three gentle turns to each side.

3. Release your fear – rub your navel with your left hand and using the thumb and forefingers of your right hand rub two points on either side of the chest (about four inches apart) directly beneath the collarbones. Then rub your navel and the points on your ribs in line with the crease in the elbow.

4. Stamp your heels, one at a time, and imagine energy moving from your left heel all the way up to your right shoulder and from your right heel to your left shoulder.

Alternatively if you are familiar with yoga it helps achieve the very same results of balance. A mixture of passive asanas/stretches (yin) combined with active stretches (yang) creates that balance. Some gurus label the yin as connective tissue and bone and the yang as the muscle tissue. Another method using the principles of acupuncture is to tap along the insides of your legs saying 'in with the yin' and then tapping the outsides of your legs saying 'out with the yang'. Repeat the same process on the inside and outer side of your arms.

MENTAL BALANCING

I have always been fascinated with the brain and its myriad of complex functions, in particular the specific functions or skill sets that are associated with the left and right hemispheres. As a left-hander, I learned from an early age that I saw things differently from right-handers, and that there were certain skills at which I excelled and others with which I struggled. For example, art and drawing came easily to me while mathematics confounded me. Later in life, I was fascinated to learn that our left hand is controlled by the right side of our brain and our right hand by the left side. In other words, left-handers are in their right mind, and vice-versa. What intrigued me the most, however, was that being left- or right-handed predisposed you to certain skill sets. In general terms, the left brain looks after logic and linear thinking while the right brain takes care of creativity and non-linear thinking. If we apply this to yin and yang, yin is the left side of the body and therefore the right hemisphere of the brain. Conversely, the right-hand side of our bodies is the masculine or yang side and so the left brain is the masculine or yang side. To reiterate:

The left side of body is controlled by the right hemisphere of the brain = yin (feminine)

The right side of the body is controlled by the left hemisphere of the brain = yang (masculine)

Almost 90 per cent of people are right-handed, therefore the majority of people are using their left brain abilities, which are yang. This may go some way towards explaining why the yang is generally more prevalent than the yin. Up to the 1970s in Ireland, children who wrote with their left hand were punished. The Catholic Church saw it as a sign of the devil. While nothing could be further from the truth, this practice gives us some insight into how the yin has been suppressed down through history. In later chapters I will delve deeper into the reasons why society has developed in this way.

Staying with the Church for a moment, labyrinths, once a common symbol of the Christian faith, can help bring balance to both hemispheres of the brain. In Chartres cathedral in France you can see the last remaining labyrinth of twenty-two labyrinths once found across Europe in major cathedrals and churches. These once formed a major part of Christian meditations. Monks walked a twelve-ring labyrinth, often on bended knees, as a symbolic representation of the journey to Jerusalem. These twelve-ring labyrinths flourished in the twelfth century, but were originally based on the Cretan labyrinths of the first century made famous by the tales of Theseus and the Minotaur.

On page 66 is a finger labyrinth. By tracing your way into the labyrinth and out again you will balance the left and right hemispheres of your mind. Your inward journey is yin and your outward journey is yang. The exercise takes you both clockwise and counter-clockwise, and establishes balance in your brain. You can approach the labyrinth with a specific question in mind. By tracing your way in and out you will activate both linear (yang) and non-linear thinking (yin), therefore drawing on all components of intelligence to answer your question. If you are the type of person who believes only in straight-line logic, you should be aware that one of the greatest scientists of the twenty-first century applauded non-linear thinking. Albert Einstein was a great proponent of abstract thought. The story goes that he was on the brink of cracking the theory of relativity when he encountered a mental roadblock and, logically, could proceed no further. Exhausted, he collapsed onto his sofa and fell asleep. He dreamt that he was riding on a photon of light that was arching and bending as he travelled. When he awoke he set to work creating mathematical equations to explain light bending. In time, this led to his equation $E=mc^2$. The chemist Friedrich Kekulé discovered the Benzene ring while daydreaming of six snakes dancing. He then made the connection that six carbon atoms could form a stable atomic structure. These are perfect examples of yin-based non-linear thinking complementing yang linear and logical thinking.[8]

Take the time to trace the labyrinth, quietly and calmly, paying close attention to your breathing as you go along. Trace in and then out first using your right hand and then your left hand. Note your observations.

How did it feel? It is interesting to note that on the journey to the centre of the labyrinth which is yin, as it is inward-moving, that you move both inward yin and outward yang, and on the return journey which is yang and outward moving, you once again find yourself moving both inwards yin and then outwards yang. This shows how physically and metaphorically we balance ourselves with inward and outward motion with yin and yang.

Practise this exercise every morning for seven days. By the end of the week, you will feel a stronger sense of intuition and mental clarity. The more you practise the greater the rewards will be. Whenever you face a difficult question use the labyrinth to help you reveal the answer. To complement this exercise, you could also use yoga breathing techniques to activate either the left or the right hemispheres of your brain, or both. Cover your left nostril and breathe in through your right nostril; this activates the left hemisphere of the brain or the logical yang side. Cover the opposite nostril and you will activate the right brain and yin or abstract thinking.

SPIRITUAL BALANCING

Of all our bodies, the spiritual is the hardest for us to access with our minds. We must therefore rely on age-old methods of communication. Almost all spiritual traditions use breathing, meditation and mantras to access a state that allows us to enter the spirit. In our quest for yin and yang balance, the greatest opportunity for enlightenment lies right under our noses. It is of course your breath. The English word spirit derives from Latin and means breath. The simple process of breathing perfectly demonstrates yin and yang. Yin, as you know, is inward moving and nourishing – this is our inhalation. The exhalation is the yang – outward moving and expansive. The two are co-dependent: one cannot exist without the other. Yang is expression and communication. Our speech can function only on the exhalation, as this is how we shape sounds into words. The inhalation, on the other hand, allows our minds time to think before formulating a response. Breath is the perfect metaphor for yin and yang as breath is life. From the day we are born to the day we die we will take hundreds of millions of breaths and with every single one we are playing out the yin yang balance. Many

Hindu traditions believe that we are all born with a certain number of breaths and heartbeats and that it is up to us how we use them in our lifetime. I have always found this concept fascinating as it begs the question, am I using my allowance of breaths for good or bad, to create happiness or sadness?

Below is a meditation that will help you tune into the natural balance of yin and yang found in nature. Select a natural setting where you will feel at ease. It could be a beach, a park, in the hills, woods or in your garden. Try to pick somewhere that gives you a strong sense of nature. If you cannot get to such a spot then simply allow your imagination to transport you to your favourite place in nature. The key to this meditation is to feel grounded.

Meditation

Sit or stand with your feet flat on the ground. Feel balanced and clear-headed. Rest your palms on your thighs. Close your eyes and become aware of your breathing. Take five deep breaths. Let each breath go down to your belly button. When you exhale, feel all the stale air in your lungs being expelled. One, breathing deeply you allow your lungs to fill ... hold for three seconds and exhale. Two, breathing deeply ... feel your lungs fill with air and hold for three seconds. Exhale deeply. Three, feel yourself relax as you breathe deeply and hold for three seconds. Exhale deeply. Four, feeling great as you inhale, hold for three seconds and exhale. Five, final deep breath, hold and exhale. Now allow your breathing to settle at a natural pace.

Become aware of the sounds around you. What sounds of nature can you hear? Become aware of them. Can you hear the sea? Can you hear the birds? Can you hear the wind in the leaves? What can you smell? Do you smell sea salt? Do you smell flowers? Do you smell grass? Notice how your body has relaxed. Now become aware of the temperature of the air. Is it warm? Is it hot? Can you feel the light breeze on your skin? Focus on this, allowing yourself to relax with each breath you take, feeling all the stress and tension leave your body with each breath. Keep breathing. Keep relaxing. Keep letting go.

Very slowly become aware of the sensation of your feet. Feel the ground beneath them. See yourself as a mighty oak tree and visualise roots growing from your feet down into the rich soil. Feel the abundance and richness of the earth surge up through the roots in your feet and into your body. Feel that you are drawing in energy through your feet and that this energy is filling you. This is the feminine energy, the yin, the energy that nourishes you. As the energy rises, visualise yourself as the oak tree in winter. As you feel the energy rise notice how you start to feel more alive. Feel how the feminine energy of the earth fills you with potential and new life.

Continuing to breathe easily, feel your branches stretch out as you visualise yourself reaching for the sky. Imagine, sense or see the sunlight streaming down onto your branches and leaves. Feel yourself in spring, growing rapidly. Feel how the sun awakens you and fills you with the masculine energy of growth, the yang energy. Feel yourself quicken as the sunlight allows thousands of leaves to burst forth forming a beautiful green canopy. Feel, sense or imagine how the masculine energy makes you reach out, fulfilling the potential of your growth.

Sense the energy of the feminine coming from the earth and the energy of the masculine coming from the sky. Feel how the two combine in perfect harmony to produce a balance of yin and yang. Feel yourself in full summer, blooming. Sense, see or imagine these energies merging to form the basis of a life-force. Feel this life-force surge through you as you radiate this energy. Feel this chi or life-force fill every cell in your body and see yourself as the mighty oak tree in full bloom.

Feel autumn coming on. Feel how the masculine energy provided the seed for your fruit. Feel how the feminine energy provided the nutrients and substance to bring life. Feel, see, sense or imagine your acorns falling from your branches and into the soil. Sense how this completes your cycle as you plant new potential life in the earth that will create your offspring. See how the oak tree represents life in perfect balance.

Say to yourself, 'I am in perfect balance with nature.'

Say, 'I am nature.'

Say, 'I am of this world and this world is of me.'

Ask your higher self, your subconscious, your spirit, or whatever you feel to be your inner self, to make you fully aware of the energy of nature, the energy of the earth, the energy of the sky. Breathe and allow this energy to flow. Let go. Surrender to the energy that is flowing into you. Feel how strong it is. What does it feel like? Where do you feel it? Can you feel it in your physical body? How does it feel in your mind? Let the sensations grow. What colour, or colours, is this energy? What does it feel like? Breathe it in, feel it wash over you. Feel the intensity of it. If the energy of nature, of mother earth, could talk what would she say to you? Would she have a message for you? Would she request you do something?

Now begin to allow yourself to return to normal, allow the energy to slip away, knowing that now you have accessed nature you can come back any time you wish. This is a special connection you have with the earth. You have experienced the wonder of the male and female energies that drive the universe and shape the natural world.

Very slowly, become aware of where you are. Allow your body and mind to return to a full state of consciousness. Five, take a deep breath and allow your body to be filled with air. Four, another deep breath and this time wiggle your fingers and toes. Three, breathe deeply once again and stretch your arms and legs. Two, another deep breath, feeling yourself fully energised and renewed, and one, fully awake.

Rest for a few moments following this relaxation and drink plenty of water. Practise the meditation seven days in a row and you will notice a mounting sense of inner calm. You may also find that your yang energy 'to do' things increases, along with your yin ability to connect with others and to see the bigger picture.

EMOTIONAL BALANCING

All emotions can be ranked along a scale, with fear residing at the negative end and love at the positive end. In between are a myriad of other emotions that range from jealousy to grief and from joy to sadness. These emotions are the messengers of the soul. They reveal a lot about what is happening in our stimulated subconsciousness and teach us about our values. Emotions are like signposts, directing us towards an understanding of why we act the way we do. They can be divided into two main categories: internally created emotions and externally stimulated emotions. Internally created emotions can arise spontaneously. They range from the joy of being surrounded by nature to feeling frustrated with yourself for losing your car keys. These emotions provide us with very good clues as to what we value and hold dear. The person who finds joy in nature will obviously have a value system that places a high priority on nature and the enjoyment of it. In the same way, if you lose your car keys and this brings on a strong negative emotion, it points to a negative belief system. It could be that you put pressure on yourself to be perfect or that you were admonished as a child for losing things. Or perhaps you try to maintain control over your life to the point where losing your keys makes you feel physically ill. By asking yourself 'Why do I feel this way?' you can explore your hidden depths and try to uncover the reasons for your actions. The more you ask this question the deeper you will travel.

EMOTIONAL MIRRORING

Externally influenced emotions paint an even clearer picture of ourselves. For example, why will Sheila's bad timekeeping drive Tom mad but have no effect on Rita? Why do some people drive you crazy at work yet your colleagues seem unaffected by them? The reason is that emotions triggered by other people work on the principle of mirroring. The reason Tom gets mad at Sheila is because he knows that he too has a propensity towards being late and he dislikes this intensely. Rita, on the other hand, does not approve of Sheila's lateness and can challenge her on it but, most importantly, does not experience a strong emotional reaction to Sheila. All of us are mirrors for one another. What you like emotionally in someone else is what you like emotionally about yourself, and vice-versa for negative traits. We tend to like or dislike that which is part of our own make-up.

So how does this relate to your yin and yang? Yin emotions are the internal emotions that arise often out of your subconscious. The yang emotions, on the other hand, are driven by your reactions to external stimuli. Another way of looking at this is that yin is introverted, meaning that the motivation or sense of self is primarily driven from the inside, while yang is extraverted. It requires external stimuli from other people to create motivation and a sense of self. To help you become aware of your emotional balance, please complete the following exercise.

EMOTIONAL JOURNALLING

By becoming more familiar with your emotions you are tuning into your emotional self and beginning to discover who you really are. At this stage it is not necessary to understand where every single emotion stems from, you have simply to become more aware of them. This process of awareness will gradually cause negative emotions to subside because you can choose to no longer allow them into your life. The positive emotions, having been recognised, begin to take up more space, developing and deepening.

Start a journal and every evening over a seven-day period list the emotions you have experienced that day, dividing them into two separate groups. Below is an example:

Internally driven emotions – yin	Externally stimulated emotions – yang
I felt anxious about the future	I felt love when my son smiled at me

I felt disconnected from life	I was angered by a friend's sharp tone
I felt exuberant while running this morning	I was annoyed about my brother not phoning me
I was grumpy when I saw rain this morning	I was delighted to get an email from an old friend
I felt really positive helping a colleague	I was proud of an achievement by my wife
I worried I wasn't good enough	I admired my boss' sense of humour

Once you have been keeping a journal for seven days you will begin to see a pattern emerging, with certain emotions reappearing on a regular basis. Analyse your feelings by asking yourself the following questions.

1. Do more emotions arise in the form of internal emotions or are they externally stimulated emotions?
2. Are your emotions more introverted or extraverted?
3. Do you notice what you dislike in others and can you find these qualities in yourself?
4. Are your emotions primarily positive or negative?
5. Are you now more emotionally aware?

By this stage you will be reaching a yin and yang balance by becoming conscious of your emotions.

The Big Yang Question

The next challenge is to list all the things you both like and dislike in other people. Think of people that you admire, like or love. What is it you love about them? Think of those you dislike. What is it about them that frustrates or annoys you? The list of things you have just described is a rough summary of your own personality. If you wish to balance your yang you must begin by eliminating the negatives and focusing on the positives.

The Big Yin Question

Examine your internal emotions by asking the five whys. Let's look at the real-life case of a client of mine. Ronnie (not his real name) came to me suffering from stress and anxiety. Having spent some time journalling he realised he was almost permanently anxious. We went through the five whys.

Me: Why are you anxious Ronnie?

Ronnie: I think it's because there is so much for me to do with work and the family, I just don't have enough time.

Me: Do you ever feel anxious Ronnie, when everything is under control or even say when you're on your holidays?

Ronnie: Actually, yes I do.

Me: So it's not always to do with workload then?

Ronnie: No.

Me: Why do you feel anxious Ronnie?

Ronnie: Well I like to be in control of everything and I worry that things might go wrong.

Me: Can you be in control of everything?

Ronnie: No I suppose not ...

Me: Then why are you worrying about things that you have no control over?

Ronnie: Emm, I just feel there won't be enough time ...

Me: Time to do what Ronnie?

Ronnie: To do it all.

Me: What is 'it all'?

Ronnie: I don't know.

Me: Of course you do Ronnie. Why do you feel you do not have enough time to do it all?

Ronnie: I think maybe I might die and I won't have done it all!

All along, Ronnie's anxiety was actually based on a fear of dying. As he later admitted, the irony was that his fear was actually creating so much anxiety that he couldn't enjoy the life he was worrying about losing. These are some of the main reasons why Ronnie developed this fear. However, they are relatively unimportant as by recognising the cost of his behaviour and emotions and understanding where they stemmed from, he became self-aware. The ego that was driving this fear subsided and his anxiety was hugely reduced as a result.

TYING IT ALL TOGETHER – COLOUR BALANCING

Through the use of colour we can unite all of these yin and yang elements. Everything in the universe has a frequency and can be measured in wavelengths. Another way to say this is that everything is held together or exists as a vibration. Colour, sound and matter all have a certain frequency or vibration. When you tune in your radio or TV you pick up the frequency of light and sound. Light has powerful healing energies. The sun for example helps us to produce vitamin D. The absence of sun can also cause depression in some people known as SAD (seasonally affected disorder). Each colour has a unique power and resonance. Many can be used to balance our yin and yang. Colour has been used for thousands of years in healing. A Hindu scientist working in America, D.P. Ghadiali (1836–1966), found that for each human organ and system, there was a particular colour that stimulated it and inhibited it. He was able to use colour to create balance in the body. In western science radio waves are used in hospitals and infra-red light treatment is also very common.[9]

On some level most of us are aware of the ability of colours to transmit energy. This is why when we are feeling depressed we wear muted colours and when we are happy we are attracted to brighter colours. Many people find that wearing the colour violet helps them balance their masculine and feminine energies. Violet is made up of the two colours at opposite ends of the spectrum, red and blue, representing masculine and feminine. In colour therapy, Reiki, art, Aura-Soma (a process of healing by applying coloured oils to the body), design and many other disciplines, the colour violet signifies clarity and unity, the coming together of mind, emotion, body and spirit. Violet has long been associated with the clergy and nobility as it is seen as denoting a higher purpose and an elevated understanding of the world.[10] In fact, in the past the lower classes were forbidden to wear this colour.

We are all affected by colours and make psychological interpretations based on them every day. Take the colour red as an example. It can be seen as aggressive or dangerous in a negative light, or confident and grounded in a positive light. It is, therefore, not difficult to understand why it represents the male energy. Blue, on the other hand, is the cool feminine energy of water, relaxation, reflection, introspection, healing and clarity.

If you want to increase your yang side or your masculine traits wear the colour red. Meanwhile, wear light blue to increase your feminine energy. Try to wear some violet and notice how it helps balance you. You could also introduce some violet into your home or workplace in the shape of flowers or include some violet food in your diet such as blueberries, aubergines, black grapes or mackerel. All of these things will have a cumulative effect on balancing your energies.

Chapter 4

Yin Yang Relationships

SWORDS AND THUNDERSTORMS

When it comes to understanding how yin and yang interact, intimate male and female relationships are perhaps the most insightful. The classic differences between the sexes and the two types of energies seem to be exaggerated when we enter the realm of attraction, love and sex. In this territory, seemingly balanced people can reveal themselves to be highly irrational and can show a side that surprises even them. The differences between how the two sexes handle arguments is perhaps the most interesting. Picture the following scene:

Kathy arrives home after a hard day at work. Nothing has gone right for her. When she got out of bed that morning she couldn't decide what to wear and cursed that she had nothing decent in her wardrobe. At work her boss announced that one of her colleagues would be leaving and that for the foreseeable future Kathy would have to cover the extra workload. In the restaurant at lunchtime the waiter spilled coffee all over her.

Meanwhile, Dave is at home waiting for Kathy to return. He has had a pretty good day and is in great form. When Kathy comes sweeping through the door like a tornado, Dave is watching TV and casually greets her. She says 'Hi' in reply but is fuming that he has not got up to welcome her. Dave continues watching TV. By now Kathy is really fuming. But she says nothing. Dave asks Kathy what she would like for dinner. In an instant she goes from what Dave perceives to be a calm state into an angry rant about 'why she always has to be the one to decide what they have for dinner'. Shocked, Dave loses his temper and storms out of the house. Outside, he finds himself suddenly calm again and wondering what had just transpired. He goes back in and apologies to Kathy for losing his temper. She is still in a foul mood and refuses to talk to him. Only now does Dave guess that she has had a really bad day and just needs some time to unwind. He lights some candles and runs her a bath. He tells her that he will go out and return with some dinner.

Later that evening, after dinner, the couple are both relaxed and content together and wonder what happened earlier in the evening.

If you take a moment to reflect on this scene it is obvious what happened. The masculine response in times of stress and anger is swift, full of energy and loud. It is a sudden, dramatic sword-like energy. In contrast, the feminine anger is like a thunderstorm. It brews slowly, all the while amassing more and more energy. Eventually, when it can no longer contain itself, it explodes, wreaking thunder and lightning, rain and wind upon its victims. These are of course the dark sides of the masculine and feminine energies. A man with a high level of feminine energy will react as Kathy did and, likewise, a woman with a lot of masculine energy will react as Dave did. It is the nature of the energy that is important, not the gender of the person.

The lesson to be learned here is how to recognise and anticipate the sword or storm so that you can then deflect it. Working on your self-awareness and understanding your partner's energy will help you to bring out the best in one another and improve your relationship. Let's look at male or yang energy first.

In its dark side, yang is the dramatic sword energy. Once a sword is drawn it must be used. Otherwise it becomes a suppressed emotion, a ticking time bomb. If we adopt the position that it is largely men who display this type of anger, then the man, in this case Dave, must release it. Dave did so by storming out and slamming the door behind him. In nature similar behaviour can be seen during the rutting season when stags and other male animals challenge each other to tests of strength. When two stags meet they size each other up. Both have the potential to kill the other but since countless dead stags would affect the herd's chances of survival the stags simply decide who is stronger and part. Later, the two animals can be seen jumping, rolling and stamping about to release the build up of testosterone-driven masculine energy. If the stags didn't do this there is a danger they might unleash their suppressed energy on the rest of the herd. Likewise, when a man goes for a run, kicks a ball, hits a baseball or a golf ball, he is releasing this energy. This is why boxing is particularly popular in disadvantaged areas where young men may be angry or frustrated with their situation. The boxing ring provides a controlled outlet for their aggression as the discipline of training and the rules of engagement impose boundaries on this energy.

The feminine energy is very different to the male. It is more of a slow burner. When its dark side is released it is spectacular. As the old saying goes, 'Hell hath no fury like a woman scorned.' The feminine anger can burn like a bushfire for days before abating. In this way it is very different from the masculine energy which is like a fireworks display, dramatic but brief. I particularly like the thunderstorm analogy for the feminine energy as it mirrors the build-up of anger. If you are interested in weather patterns you become adept at recognising the signs of an impending storm. As clouds gather on the horizon, they gain energy from the heat and moisture that is rising up from the land. If this continues unchecked then a storm will occur. However, unlike the yang energy that needs to be released quickly, if the yin heat and moisture abate then so too will the storm. If Dave had noticed the signs earlier and welcomed Kathy home then the storm could have been averted. Equally, Kathy could have noticed that the conditions for a storm were ripe and taken measures to avoid it. By reading an enjoyable book or taking a stroll in the park she could also have stopped the storm brewing. However, once a storm commences it can rain for hours until all the energy in the clouds is spent. Likewise, it can take the feminine energy much longer to dissipate and blow over. Dave's act of lighting some candles and running a bath was the perfect way of handling the situation as it allowed Kathy to slowly unwind and release her energy.

Once both partners in a relationship are aware of the kind of conditions that give rise to a storm they can be more careful in the future. After all, prevention is better than cure. We all have dark sides to our yin and yang and they must be recognised and accepted. If they are not managed, they have the potential to sabotage even the best relationships. If you are serious about tackling the negative states that you or your partner are prone to, then make sure to complete the exercise at the end of this chapter.

So how do our masculine and feminine traits influence who we are attracted to? Put quite simply, opposites attract. Energy will seek to find balance and harmony. If a man is 60 per cent male energy and 40 per cent female energy then his ideal partner will be a woman who is 60 per cent female energy and 40 per cent male. In this way, the union will represent 100 per cent of each type of energy. The danger lies in two people coming together who have similar excesses of either male or female energy. If the couple have too much yang, they will have a very active relationship but the intimate and nurturing side will be lacking. The other dark side of this mix is that you would have two people with high levels of ego or aggression. This is a recipe for disaster. Relationships with high levels of feminine energy are equally volatile. They are typically high in intimacy and communication but completely lacking in action or structure. In their darker side, such relationships tend to be bitchy and manipulative. If you think of couples you know in your own life who ultimately did not work out, what was the balance like in their relationships?

As we can see, each energy type needs to find balance in its opposite. It is the dynamic difference between the two energies that creates success in relationships. One of the greatest challenges for modern society lies in understanding these rules of attraction. Currently, western society seems intent on homogenising men and women. This is resulting in total chaos. Many men have become so metrosexual that they are almost more female than their female partners. Meanwhile, women are being led to believe that they must be as tough as men to progress in life. The upshot is that the very energy that has attracted men to women and women to men for eons is disappearing. The result is mismatched relationships between two people who are not really who they claim to be. Both sexes must be true to their natural energy. To go against it is to deny millions of years of evolution. I am not advocating stereotypes – that all men should work on building sites and all women rear children – but rather that both sexes should be proud of their uniqueness.

In a nutshell, to find your perfect match you must look for someone with the opposite balance of your energy. You'll know when you have found this person as the dynamic and magnetic energy between you will be unmistakable. All natural laws operate on this principle: minus and plus joining together. This is the basic concept of physics. Molecules are bound together by the fact that they contain positively charged protons and negatively charged electrons. Think of a magnet. Each side has a positive or a negative charge. If you try and put two positives together they repel one another. The same happens with two negatives. However, place a negative alongside a positive and the two will be drawn together. Relationships operate in the same way. This is the essence of the law of attraction. Yin attracts yang, and vice-versa. This law holds our universe together and, likewise, our relationships. Therefore, by being yourself and allowing others to see your natural energy, you will attract your balancing force.

In Chapter 2 we discussed anima and animus archetypes. Jung believed these archetypes existed within all of us. In a woman, the animus includes the perfect lover. In a man, the anima is the female archetype of his perfect lover. Another way to look at this is that we are born as one half of a perfect person. Many spiritual traditions speak of an *anam cara* or soul mate. All of us are looking for our soul mate or perfect partner and the way we identify them is that we recognise the completing part of our soul in the other person. By being our true selves and getting in touch with our archetypes we can become more aware of what type of mate we are seeking. Jung believed that we go through life seeking our anima or animus, and that this archetype was largely shaped by the relationship we had with our parent of the opposite sex. If our childhood experiences with this parent were positive then we will look for the traits they possess in a prospective partner. Unfortunately, the same applies if we had a negative relationship with this parent; we will seek partners who demonstrate the same negative traits. This explains history's tendency to repeat itself and why, for example, a woman with an abusive father might go on to marry an abusive man. Jungian psychologists would take this theory a step further and argue that men spend their lives searching for the traits of their mothers and women searching for the traits of their fathers. Children who have been abandoned by a parent sometimes spend their lives seeking to replace that lost parent through other relationships. For example, a young boy who has been abandoned by his mother may be unable to hold on to a relationship as an adult because he is constantly chasing after the elusive archetype of his mother. He is not familiar with his mother's energy, and therefore his anima, so he may enter into relationships with partners who are completely unsuitable.

Alongside the emotional and subconscious elements, attraction also has a very physical side to it. We must look to evolution and the survival of the fittest to understand how this works. On the most primal level, a female with large breasts, a narrow waist and wide hips visually represents a potentially fertile mate with all the necessary attributes to bear and nurture children. Female gorillas saw their ideal mate in a silver-backed male gorilla with a narrow waist, a V-shaped back, broad shoulders and a broad chest, all of which suggested he was fit, strong and capable of fathering children. These shapes evolved via a process of survival of the fittest, with evolution deciding which were the most likely to produce and rear children successfully. Nowadays, male world leaders, members of sports teams, etc., mimic this yang shape.

Many male heads of state, regardless of their body shape, dress in suits with shoulder pads, narrow-cut waists and double-breasted lapels that mirror the classic silver-back V shape. In advance of the 2003 Rugby World Cup, the victorious England team had special jerseys designed that featured V shapes on the arms, chest, back and shoulders. This pattern created an optical illusion with the man appearing bigger than he actually was.

In the case of women, they employ push-up bras, corsets and various other fashion tricks to recreate the archetypal feminine body shape. All of this is aimed at attracting the right mate. An interesting twist, however, is the current trend of waif-like models that represent a definite shift away from the fuller female shape. Yang energy lies at the heart of this trend. This may come as a surprise since the fashion industry is mostly aimed at women. Slim bodies show off the clothes better and the designers want the audience to look at the clothes and not the model. If this is the case then clothes become more important than the woman herself and the by-product of this is that many women think skinny equals style. If this is indeed the case in modern women's fashion, then such trends are only adding to the already confused state of male/female attraction. Countless surveys indicate that men prefer women of a fuller shape rather than the boyish waifs of the catwalk. However, powerful and influential marketing campaigns are in essence encouraging women to pursue male-like figures. This suggests that our social and cultural mix may be unbalanced and not fully representative of the feminine yin energy.

Sex is a very powerful force in our society today. The masculine sex drive is very ancient in nature; it is the kill it, have sex with it, eat it primal drive. It is driven by a biological impetus to procreate with as many females as possible. That is not to say that all men act on this impulse, but it may be there in the background. The female sex drive is equally ancient but it is more about intimacy, nurturing, sensuality and closeness. Which of the two sex drives do you think dominates western society? It is quite obviously the male view of sex and this is largely due to advertising and the media. All you need do is turn on a TV or walk down a street with billboards in most cities and you will find the masculine sex drive everywhere. It is much more difficult to find its softer opposite, the female sex drive. Once again, this highlights how society has become very masculine in its energy. But too much of anything can be bad and a balance of the two sex drives is required for harmony and equilibrium.

So if a masculine approach to sex dominates our society, what are the implications for our relationships? I once read a great quote that stated, 'Men use intimacy to get sex and women use sex to get intimacy.' While life may not be quite that black and white, this quote gives us insight into the nature of the masculine and feminine drives. Partners can sometimes withhold intimacy or sex as a means of controlling a relationship. But, as always, it comes down to balance. Each partner must experience and deliver both intimacy and physical sex. This creates equilibrium in the yin yang interaction.

Sex is also surrounded by a huge amount of societal conditioning. While some cultures create a guilt complex, such as the Catholic Ireland of old, others promote promiscuous behaviour. Britain topped the list in an international study based on one night stands and how comfortable those questioned were with casual sex.[11] The promotion of sex in music videos, films, video games and glossy magazines in the western world is very much masculine in view. Women are all too often portrayed as sex objects and men as mindless fools. Unfortunately, this has a spin-off effect on the behaviour and attitudes of people, teenagers in particular. Instead of becoming aware of their own sexuality and internal balance, young people are emulating the role models they see on screen. It is no wonder that later in life many of them struggle to find balanced and harmonious relationships. Think about it. Have your own attitudes or sexual behaviour been affected by the media or the role models around you? What about your partner?

With all this talk about sex we could hardly neglect to mention the most amazing aspect of it – and what serves as the simplest expression of the masculine and feminine energies. We are of course talking about the role of sperm and eggs. The sperm, which obviously represent the masculine energy, are programmed to do just one thing – swim, swim and then swim some more. The egg on the other hand, representing the feminine, simply sits still and waits for the sperm to come to her. What happens on a macro level is not all that different to what happens on a micro level. Women make themselves attractive to draw men in, while men then pursue their chosen woman.

SAME-SEX RELATIONSHIPS

If you are reading this as a gay man or woman you may think that this view relates only to heterosexual relationships. For the purpose of example it does. However, these energies play out in the exact same way in heterosexual and homosexual relationships. One person will always be more yin and one more yang. Or both may exhibit equal levels of these energies, in which case attraction, rows and compatibility will ensue just as they do in heterosexual relationships. Transgender relationships, however, are more complicated. A person may be born male but have an overwhelming sense that their emotions, mind and spirit are yin in energy. Likewise, a person may be born female but experience an overwhelming yang energy. I cannot hypothesise a reason for this inverted energy balance; all I can say is that I know it occurs. Some of our ancestors treated these people in a very special way. The North American Indians considered them wise, believing that they offered a unique perspective on the world, being able to see it from two points of view. Undoubtedly, however, in many societies they faced the same discrimination as they do today. The joker archetype, mentioned in Chapter 2, is believed to often alternate between genders and sexual persuasions.

Regardless of your sexual persuasion it is important to identify not only your own yin and yang balance but also that of your partner or potential partner. If you are already in a relationship, are you and your partner aware of your individual sexual energy and how much yin (intimacy) or yang (sex) you both require? Until you know this you may be harbouring expectations that cannot be met and this will lead to frustration and problems down the line. If you and your partner can find balance in your yin and yang energies then the success of your relationship has millions of years of evolution and the laws of physics on its side.

Soul Mates

Another concept worth exploring is that of the soul mate or *anam cara* as it is known in Gaelic, meaning soul friend. So what are soul mates and how do they fit into the yin and yang concept? Soul mates share a spiritual connection. They can be someone you are in a relationship with or simply someone with whom you have an incredibly deep connection

– a connection that you may not always understand but that exists nonetheless. In mysticism the soul mate is your other half. Many traditions talk of reuniting the soul – one half being masculine and yang, and the other being feminine and yin. Some eastern traditions maintain that you travel with this soul through many lifetimes, sometimes as family, sometimes as enemies and sometimes as lovers, but always as two halves of the one whole, each teaching the other life lessons that will eventually lead to reunification. I believe that yin and yang help us to attract a compatible partner but the fire that ignites these relationships goes beyond simple attraction. It comes down to love. Love is the supreme energy that breathes life and passion into the yin yang complex. The following verses from the ancient *The Song of Solomon* speak of the journey of love, the soul and the spirit:

The Song of Solomon

2:8   The voice of my beloved!
      Behold, he comes,
      leaping on the mountains,
      skipping on the hills.

2:9   My beloved is like a roe or a young hart.
      Behold, he stands behind our wall!
      He looks in at the windows.
      He glances through the lattice.

2:10 My beloved spoke, and said to me,
      'Rise up, my love, my beautiful one, and come away.

2:11 For, behold, the winter is past.
      The rain is over and gone.

2:12 The flowers appear on the earth.
      The time of the singing has come,
      and the voice of the turtledove is heard in our land.

2:13 The fig tree ripens her green figs.
      The vines are in blossom.
      They give forth their fragrance.
      Arise, my love, my beautiful one,
      and come away.'

8:6   Set me as a seal on your heart,
      as a seal on your arm;
      for love is strong as death.
      Jealousy is as cruel as Sheol.
      Its flashes are flashes of fire,
      a very flame of the Lord.

8:7   Many waters can't quench love,
      neither can floods drown it.

                    Extract taken from the World English Bible
                                         (www.ebible.org)

This extract encapsulates the ancient dance of the masculine and feminine. While more commonly found in the *New Jerusalem Bible* used by many Christians, the song forms a very strong part of the mystic traditions associated with the Jewish Qabalah. It is interesting to decode the verses which have in them the elements of fire in 'flash of fire', air in 'my dove', earth in 'the mountains' and water in 'flood'. As we have seen, yin and yang are also represented by the four elements, with water and earth being yin and fire and air being yang. It is believed that the song was originally a liturgical litany for performance during rites of sacred marriage (the *hieros gamos*). It is very similar to the love poetry of the ancient fertility religions practised in Sumer, Cannan and Egypt.[12]

In our exploration of the attraction between yin and yang, one very simple rule emerges – be yourself. Whether you are in a relationship or looking for one, by allowing your true energy to be seen you will attract the right person into your life.

Chapter 5

The Business of Yin and Yang

ANCIENT ROME ECHOES IN THE BOARDROOM AND ON THE FACTORY FLOOR

You might be wondering how the yin and yang balance fits into the world of business. These energies also exist in industry especially in the western world where business is the very centrepiece of our society. In many cases, our lives and those of our family and friends are built around our careers and professional aspirations. It is important, however, to understand both the underlying energy that drives your business attitude and that of the other businesses with which you deal. As you may already have guessed, most western businesses are yang in nature. In many instances, they reside very firmly on the dark side of the masculine energy, their insatiable appetites for power and expansion driving them to conquer, plunder and pillage.

To find the forerunner of the modern company we must

look to ancient Rome. Ancient Roman culture represented the zenith of a major departure from traditional beliefs around male and female balance that had started with the Greeks. Women spent their lives under the control of men, be it their fathers or their husbands. They were not allowed to hold office or make suggestions on matters of governance.[13] This period of western history represents the greatest repression of the values and strengths of the yin energy.

The yang approach persists today. The structure of modern businesses closely mirrors that of Ancient Rome. The chairman of the board is the emperor, or Julius Caesar; the board are the senators; the managers are the generals; the assistant managers are the centurions; the workers are the foot soldiers; and the shareholders are the citizens of Rome. It is remarkable how this style of governance has penetrated almost every type of business in the western world. Our modern political system is similarly structured. Just look at the United States of America with its House of Representatives, its president and its senators. It is a modern-day Rome. The citadel, the White House and much of Washington DC's architecture is a direct stylistic reference to Rome, complete with Roman pillars and expansive marbled halls. A time-travelling Roman could be forgiven if he mistook Washington DC for an evolved latter-day Rome.

The first-century Roman Empire marks a definite and

major shift in yin and yang forces, away from balance and towards a structure defined by man for man. The suppression of the feminine during this time still has ripple effects today. Not only did it lead to centuries of discrimination against women but it also stifled the feminine energy of men. The business world, above any other area of society, has perpetuated this imbalance of yin and yang.

Most of us are unaware of the extent to which we are influenced by ancient Rome. Take our Gregorian calendar for example. It was first introduced in 1582, taking over from Caesar's Julian calendar which had been in use since 45 BC. Prior to the Julian calendar, society was tuned into nature and into the lunar cycles, with the full moon denoting the middle of the month and signalling the time for seeds to be sown or harvests to be reaped. This system was essentially feminine in nature as it worked with the natural rhythms of the planet and was mirrored by the female menstrual cycle. Newgrange, a megalithic tomb in County Meath that was built in 3200 BC, is a perfect example of how our ancestors marked the passage of time. On the shortest day of the year, the winter solstice, the sun shines directly through a small slit above the doorway of this tomb and illuminates the burial chamber. The Celts believed this event marked the end of winter and the beginning of the return of light. The darkness and the chamber represented the womb and winter (the yin) and the shaft of light represented the seed of man and the summer (yang). This tomb shows how our ancestors integrated the moon and the sun into their belief in the balance and unity of the masculine and feminine.

So why then did the Romans decide to move away from a system that was so in tune with nature? Julius Caesar was responsible for the shift. Caesar had an insatiable appetite for world domination, but there was one main obstacle standing in his path. If he was to harness the power of Roman citizens far and wide then he needed a more accurate time and dating system. He could then demand that on 30 June such and such had to travel to Londinium or Athens or Alexandria. The advent of the Julian calendar marked the end of a calendar defined by nature and a move towards a man-made system that rewarded Caesar with control over huge areas of land and millions of subjects. This philosophy of control led to the expansion of the Roman Empire. In fact, the Romans were so successful at empire building (success being a yang trait) that they essentially overtraded. They grew too big too quickly. While trying to maintain the boundaries of an ever-increasing empire, they left themselves vulnerable to attack from neighbouring Germanic tribes from the north who eventually overran them. The Roman legacy lives on today in many shapes and sizes, one of these being modern western business.

The Industrial Revolution was the next major milestone in the suppression of the yin in the world of business. Agriculture and small craft-based industries were plunged into a new world of mechanisation and, while industrialisation brought many advantages, it also brought its share of disadvantages. One of these was the exploitation of workers as machines gradually became more valuable than the people operating them. Little has changed in the twenty-first century. Like the Roman period, the Industrial Revolution still affects how we do business today.

You may be wondering how any of this suppresses the feminine? Around the time of the Industrial Revolution, accounting classified machines as assets and people as overheads, making it clear where businesses considered their value to lie. The people in a business represent the yin and the machines represent the yang. When machines are deemed to be of greater value than people, the yang moves to the forefront, obscuring the yin.

If you take the world we live in, people, businesses, nature, art, music and almost anything else you can think of work best where there is balance. If we apply the same logic to business in the western world, do we find this balance? Of course we don't. Do we find expansionism matched by nurturing? Do we find profiteering matched by social contribution? Do we find the rights of the family matched by those of the career? Do we find that the generation of pollution and waste is equal to the amount of conservation and environmentalism? Do we see yin balanced by yang? You know the answer to all of these questions only too well – no. Modern-day western businesses represent the pinnacle of the imbalance in our world. The general attitude seems to be, 'We would like to respect people, families, the environment and society but making a profit is more important.' But as the ancient saying goes, 'you reap what you sow', and it is only now that it is beginning to dawn on us how badly we have been running our businesses.

Industry, in its current form, is killing us. It couldn't be more serious. Stress is linked to six of the most common causes of death in the United States today: heart disease, cancer, lung ailments, accidents, cirrhosis of the liver and suicide. Vast volumes of research reinforce this link. What is more is that this figure is rising as our levels of stress continue to climb. A Roper Starch Worldwide Inc. report showed that 'globally, 23 per cent of women executives and professionals, and 19 per cent of their male peers, say they feel "super-stressed".'[14] Stress has a dramatic effect not only on the physical health of the worker, but also on their emotional, mental and spiritual health. Job burnout rates are spiralling. People in every industry, from teaching to medicine to law, are buckling under the pressure. This type of toxic economy is ultimately unsustainable.

Stress affects more than just the worker. It affects the entire family as the stressed individual becomes so disconnected from their true self that they struggle to maintain relationships. Their children have role models who are constantly tired, irritable and unhappy. This has a profound effect on the well-being of the developing child. Through my work as a life and business coach, I meet people every day who have lost a meaningful connection with their family. They work so hard that they rarely see their loved ones and during the little time they do spend with them, they are too tired to enjoy their company. The irony is that if you ask these people why they work so hard they will usually tell you they do it for their families, to ensure that they have the best opportunities in life.

It should be clear by now that the nurturing and caring aspect of the feminine yin traits are almost completely absent in the business world. The simple fact is that the family unit is of little or no importance to the majority of companies. But like most things that lack balance, this system will eventually collapse. Overworked executives will walk away from the traditional ways of doing business and, when they do, they will leave in large numbers. People are already beginning to demand change, but the business culture has a very long way to go.

During a session with one of my clients, a very successful career banker, he confided in me that the stress and hectic pace of business life were having negative effects on his family. Contrary to what you may be expecting, however, this is not the predictable story of the hard-working man with no time to spend with his wife and children. Let me tell you about Kevin's (not his real name) situation.

Kevin came to me looking for professional coaching to help him achieve a work/life balance. As usual, I started by helping him break his life down into several key areas and then assessing how he was doing in each of these. To both our surprise, Kevin was doing really well in time spent with his children and friends and at sports and hobbies – all areas that most high-powered business executives often neglect. When our discussion moved on to his relationship with his wife, I could see the tears well up in Kevin's eyes. He confessed, 'She is lost and I don't know her anymore.'

He went on to explain that his wife Liz (again not her real name) was also a banker, but that she felt a constant need to be in control and was unable to let go of her work. She divided most of her time between long hours in the office and business trips abroad. She had started at the bottom rung of the company ladder and worked her way up to the role of senior executive. But she now lived in constant fear that there was someone lurking in the wings, ready to take her place and all that she had worked so hard to earn. This paranoia spilled over into her evenings and weekends, which she spent writing reports, making phone calls and reading emails. Kevin related how her Blackberry had become a permanent fixture beside their bed lest she receive an urgent midnight email. Liz was so exhausted that she was relying on energy bars and drinks to keep her alert. Their children no longer felt like they had a mother and Kevin felt like he no longer had a wife. When I asked him why he thought his wife was going to such extremes, he answered that she wanted to ensure she had a great pension down the line and could spend lots of time with Kevin and their three children. I didn't need to point the irony out to Kevin. Liz may very well no longer have a family by the time she retires or, even worse, may not even see it to retirement age.

Perhaps you recognise a little of yourself in Liz or know someone who resembles her. What drives us to work crazy hours and miss out on seeing our families, friends and loved ones? Why can't we see the importance of living life today when we have no guarantee that there will be a tomorrow? Liz is clearly the victim of a system that does not have room for the feminine. Her colleagues know her as a 'ball-breaker' – someone you don't mess with. Does she sound like someone who has balanced her masculine and feminine energies? Liz and Kevin are not unique. They are the products of a modern working culture that suppresses the feminine in both men and women. The sad reality for Liz is that on the day she retires her bank will quickly find a replacement and forget all about her. Within a few weeks people will ask, 'Liz who?' Yet Liz is sacrificing everything – her health, her happiness and her family – for a company that sees her as just another faceless cog in the wheel.

In my work I often use a technique called deathbed thinking to help my clients put their careers into perspective. The premise is simple. Imagine that you are at the end of your days and are looking back on your life. What will you value most? What difference will you have made to the world? What will you have contributed? For most people, this sobering and eye-opening exercise boils down to simple things, like having been a great parent or having made a difference to their community. No one who is really honest with themselves will answer, 'It was great the way I made all that money' or 'It was great the way I dedicated my life to a company that never cared about me.' If you were at the end of your days what could you say you had achieved? What would you like to be able to say? Will your life have been well spent?

One of the reasons why we allow work to consume us in the western world can be traced back to our education system. Education and business are intrinsically linked in the West. We teach our children skills to make them useful in the workplace. These tend to be left-brained yang skills such as mathematics, reading, writing, science, business studies and languages all of which are very important and useful. From an early age these are also the skills that are rewarded in the form of praise from teachers and parents. Again, this is a good thing. Where the imbalance occurs, however, is that our yin sides, the right-hand sides of our brain that deals with philosophy, art, music, creativity, emotional insight, drama, healing, caring and intuition, are neglected. The right-hand side is the 'poor cousin' of the left brain whose skill set is perceived to be more valuable to business. This means that we are conditioned to expect rewards for the skills of the yang or left brain while the yin skills of the right brain are seen as an indulgence. Our education system is therefore discouraging children from exploring their full range of abilities. No wonder many young adults find themselves lost when they enter the workforce and are forced to try to adapt themselves to the very narrow profile demanded by so many businesses.

IQ vs EQ

A telling indicator of the way the business world perceives people lies in its emphasis on IQ (intelligence quotient) over EQ (emotional quotient). While IQ is yang in nature, EQ is yin. If we look at how businesses recruit their employees we will find that IQ tests prevail. IQ tests were first used in 1904 by the psychologist Alfred Binet who was commissioned by the French government to come up with a system of measuring and grading a child's intelligence. It was the government's intention to build special schools for the children who scored poorly on these tests and were in need of remedial help. This test, and others like it, was used by various institutions throughout the century to neatly label people and put them 'in a box'. This purely yang way of measuring people does not take into account the intelligence of emotion. Today, emotional intelligence is recognised as one of the key factors in achieving success in the workplace. As Daniel Goleman, author of *Emotional Intelligence*, puts it, '67 per cent of the abilities needed for effective performance were EI (emotional intelligence) competencies, and IQ (intelligence quotient) accounts for only about 25 per cent of job success'. Even when the evidence is clearly presented, many businesses still overlook the importance of emotional intelligence and people skills, with one of my own clients referring to it as 'flowery stuff'.

But the reality could not be further from the truth. Some of the most successful people in the world never attended college. Instead, they used their emotional intelligence to excel in their chosen field. Nelson Mandela, Mother Teresa and Gandhi all used their emotional abilities to unite people and change the world. Many business leaders boast that they started out with nothing but by putting their emotional intelligence to work they met with great success. Hugely successful entrepreneurs such as Sir Richard Branson, Walt Disney, Coco Chanel, Michael Dell, Steve Jobs and Bill Gates, all either failed to finish college, dropped out or never started.[15] None of them required an MBA to be successful, yet some quarters would argue that it is essential if you want to achieve business success. The real secret to success in your chosen career is a balance of both cognitive intellect (yang) and emotional intelligence (yin).

If we look at the systems in place in our society we can see that from a very young age our parents, our schools and our colleges are all grooming us to work in a yang-orientated business culture that neglects the feminine aspects of our characters. The system is inherently flawed. A perfect illustration of this is the Irish health system. In Ireland we recruit doctors through a system known as the CAO system of points. Our final exams on finishing school are called the leaving cert, which is by and large a memory test based on what you can remember and recall. This means that those with the best memories often score the highest points and get the places on the medical courses. At no stage are the potential doctors and specialists assessed for their emotional abilities or their empathy. We could be missing some brilliant doctors because they cannot achieve the very high points. What we are doing is recruiting yang people to a yin system. Healthcare should be about caring and creating a patient first culture. Yet some yang-orientated doctors and consultants see themselves as the most important part of the system and approach their work with an attitude of ego rather than empathy. That said, many doctors and healthcare professionals are very caring and kind. Interestingly Malcolm Gladwell in his book *Tipping Point* quotes research that shows in America the doctors who spend the most amount of time at the bedside of their clients are sued the least – proof that an empathy-based approach is worthwhile. As I write this there are thankfully moves underway to put in place an aptitude test to help assess the suitability of a person to a career in medicine in Ireland.

The larger question we need to ask ourselves about business is what balance do we want? Who do we want to work with? I use a tool in my business work called a CPQ or Craft Personality Questionnaire. One of its measurement metrics of the personality of a employee is a measure of their empathy and ego. As we know ego is yang and empathy is yin. If I find a team that has all what I like to call 'farmers' – high empathy but low drive – then the team will struggle, as there is not enough drive to compete. On the other hand if there are too many yang characters, or as I refer to them 'warriors', then there is not a caring attitude or place for people in the company. Either extreme is a bad thing. Just like the civilisations of old, the warriors need the farmers and the farmers need the warriors. The best teams I work with are those with a strong balance of both yin and yang, masculine and feminine, warrior and farmer. Think about the business you work in – how many are warriors how many are farmers?

How do we create the Balance?

Until businesses make a concerted effort to bring about a balance of yin and yang, their workplaces will remain little more than prisons without walls. These prisons are full of unhappy inmates leading soulless existences for a three-week annual holiday, money and a rap on the knuckles every time they fail to meet their targets. If this grim situation is to be rectified, it will require the courage and vision of a new kind of corporate leader. I believe it is possible for companies to achieve a balance of yin and yang and become supportive and enlightening workplaces; companies that manage to thrive and grow but not at the expense of their workers' well-being. How refreshing would it be to see an annual report that speaks not only about an increase in the company's turnover but also about an increase in the happiness of its workforce as a result of the introduction of a new health programme or some other such initiative.

Looking at your own workplace, do you think there is a balance of yin and yang? If you work for a non-profit philanthropic organisation then you may find your business is yin. In other words, the business works for the betterment of people. Likewise, if you work for a company that exploits its workers to increase its profits then there will be a surplus of yang energy. Or you may be working in an organisation that has a yang deficiency and suffers from a lack of structure and organisation, meaning that nothing ever gets done. Does your company strive to balance the well-being of its staff with its need to turn a profit? If so you are working in a well-balanced business.

I am in no doubt that the US subprime mortgage crisis, which triggered the collapse of the banking system and a global economic recession, is based on nothing more than pure yang greed. Billions were loaned by banks to people who would never be able to repay their debts. The only objective of these banks was profit. As sometimes happens, synchronistically, while thinking about the role of the banks in the crisis as I sat in my car outside my local bank, I heard a related story on the radio. Almost as if we were on the same wavelength I heard a contributor on the show brilliantly express how recently a friend had told her the story of a meeting with her bank manager. When the bank manager was doing a financial review for her friend, he accused her of being seriously under borrowed!

No wonder people were sucked into the credit trap when banks were in my opinion reckless in trying to achieve their own bonuses by hitting lending targets that could not in reality result in all those debts being paid off. The thinking was short term and driven by the banking top brass who wanted their bonuses and pensions in the next three years and who really did not care about the medium- to long-term consequences to the bank, the shareholders, the staff and most importantly the customer. This was yang business gone mad. The restraint and the calm of the yin was just not present. Some blame must also be levelled at the borrowers: they were fuelled by the same yang drive for more and did not use their yin sense of balance and caution. However, as we will see in coming chapters, if society is mostly yang-based then we are encouraged to expand, risk it all, be brave and even reckless.

As we can see, nature has found a way of restoring balance to this sector. The pendulum is swinging back. Many of the top bankers responsible for the current economic crisis are now unemployed and those who never invested time in their lives outside the bank are suffering. I know of one top banker who was described to me by a friend of his as 'a broken man and a shadow of his former self'. Their identities are intertwined with their high-profile, ego-driven careers and, unless they can learn to embrace their yin energy, they will struggle to rebuild their lives. The governments and the people no longer trust or believe the banks and this is their greatest loss. I would like to believe that those now running the banks will have learned their lesson, but I fear that will not have and may never. The yang quest and the greed is too strong and too attractive. However, this does not stop you from deciding to be balanced and through the power of one we can all help create the change required.

Use the chart following to score your employer or business. Allow one mark for each description that corresponds with your business. Feel free to add your own factors to the list. At the end, add up your score to see if your business is yin or yang in nature. The ideal result would be a high yang score matched by an equally high yin score. This simple exercise will give you an indication of where your company or organisation needs improvement:

Yang Factors	*Yin Factors*
Finance	**Finance**
1. The company is profitable	1. The company donates to charity
2. Employee earnings are fair	2. Bonuses for teamwork
3. Suppliers are paid on time	3. Invests in people development
People	**People**
4. Teaches technical skills	4. Cares about employee happiness
5. Provides good working structures	5. Respects family/work balance
6. Motivates and is high in energy	6. Educates in soft skills and people skills
Social/Ethical	**Social/Ethical**
7. Acts with integrity	7. Cares for the environment
8. Has sports and social provisions	8. Supports local community
9. Supports pension and health cover	9. Supports ethical trade (fair trade)
Total	**Total**

Yang 7-9 – excellent   Yin 7-9 – excellent
Yang 4-6 – OK   Yin 4-6 – OK
Yang 1-3 – change jobs!   Yin 1-3 – change jobs!

Chapter 6

The Yin Yang Society

A Long and Winding Road

To understand modern-day western society we must first understand why it has evolved as it has. The roots of western society can be traced back to the Greek, Roman and Christian civilisations, each of which was built one on top of the other. The Greeks came first and developed a philosophy that the Romans later built upon, adding laws into the fray. Then came the Christians who united law and philosophy with religion. In the West we have a combination of the Greco, Roman and Christian cultures that has been influenced at various stages, but to a lesser degree, by Jewish, Celtic, Coptic (Egyptian), Slavic and Islamic aspects of philosophy, law, religion and science. Many of the older civilisations such as the old Jewish and Celtic cultures would have fostered a strong sense of the feminine, but little of that has pervaded to western culture of today. Interestingly, these other cultures have had the least impact on societies where the yin or feminine characteristics are strong. Meanwhile, the cultures that comprise our foundation are acutely yang, with a fierce patriarchal bias that lacks a balancing yin or matriarchal force. The modern western world, which includes Europe and the various countries colonised by the Europeans, such as the US, Australia and Latin America, all display this staunch yang bias. We also see this bias in Islamic and Russian society, and to a lesser extent in China and India. A yang culture of expansionism, commercialism and unchecked growth dominates our world. However, these are not just western characteristics; China and India are two of the fastest-growing economies in the world and have massive appetites for resources and wealth. The implications this yang bias has on our world are immense and I will deal with them in the next chapter.

If we accept that western society is predominantly yang in energy, what does this mean for us westerners? It means that we have only half the picture; we are flying with one wing. In earlier chapters, we saw how this imbalance affects people personally, in work and in their relationships. These are the external consequences of a crisis that has its origins at a much deeper level.

If you think of western society as a house, imagine that cracks are appearing in the foundations supporting it. If the foundations give way, then the walls, the roof and everything else in the house will follow suit. The roof is a metaphor for all of us, the walls are the environment and the contents of the house are our families and possessions, the foundations are our core belief systems and spirituality, and where our sense of yin and yang resides. Our future is hanging in the balance. As Al Gore said in his documentary on global warming, *An Inconvenient Truth*, 'Our ability to live is what is at stake.' If we were to compare society to a computer we would see that the operating system is fundamentally flawed and any attempt to run a programme on it would cause the hard-drive to crash. With this kind of an operating system in place, it is no wonder our personal lives, our families and our businesses frequently flounder. We are running the wrong software. Until we become aware of this we are doomed to repeat the same mistakes over and over again. As the old adage goes, 'If you keep doing what you've always done, then you'll keep getting what you've always got.'

Has the human race ever had the right balance? Have we ever had the right operating system? Thankfully, the answer is yes. At some stage or another during their development, all of the ancient cultures had a balance of yin and yang, with patriarchy equalling matriarchy. The earliest evidence of this can be found in the Babylonian creation myth, 'Enuma Elish'. It speaks of the battle between Marduk (the masculine) and Tiamat (the feminine). Over time the ancient cultures were either invaded by yang cultures or grew increasingly yang-orientated and expansionist of their own accord. It is like these cultures failed to realise the benefits of balance and the yang, which always has a louder voice, seemed to push to the forefront and suppress the feminine.

Western society has flirted with yin and yang at various stages, but the latter has generally emerged as the more seductive of the two. The closest any society has come to getting it right was during the golden ages of the ancient Chinese, Indians, Mayans, Babylonians, Egyptians and Celts. All of these societies, which came into being virtually independent of one another's influence, believed in the necessity for balance between the masculine and the feminine. For a time, these societies were balanced and prospered. It was only when the yang took over and whetted the appetite for expansion that these societies were invaded and conquered by other yang nations. However, the efforts they made towards achieving balance serves as a valuable legacy that can teach us a great deal.

To discover how we managed to move so far away from the feminine, or the yin, we must travel back to ancient Greece. The word philosophy derives from Greek and translates as 'lover of Sophia' – Sophia being the Greek goddess of wisdom. She represented feminine wisdom and knowledge of how to live a good life; she was the opposite power to the masculine yang. But Plato, Sophia's lover, fell in love with Logos, or what we know today as logic. This shift from Sophia to Logos represented a move towards the masculine, and a resultant denigration of Sophia's wisdom. From then on, the Greeks and later the Roman and Christian empires would move further and further away from Sophia and towards Logos. This was the equivalent of denying the right-hand side of our brains, the home of creativity, imagination and intuition, and focusing exclusively on the left-hand side. The left-hand logical hemisphere of the brain is time-bound, in that it is very conscious and aware of time. The intuitive right-hand side of the brain does not process time in the same way; in fact it seems to operate outside of time. That is to say it has no awareness of time. For example when we play music, paint or draw, socialise with friends we can completely forget about time. I have certainly experienced this many times while painting. As a result, our right brain is under-developed in comparison to the left 'logical' hemisphere.

In Ireland, our ancestors emerged from the Mesolithic period, or Middle Stone Age, around 8000 BC, with a strong connection to nature. They lived off the land and witnessed first-hand nature's dependency on cycles and balance. They were a deeply spiritual people and connected everything to a careful balancing of the masculine and the feminine. Their belief system was known as Druidism. Druids were spiritual people who trained in the arts of homeopathy, herbal remedies, healing and knowledge of the higher realms. Their role was to counsel, guide and advise, and alongside the poets and bards (musicians), they taught the culture and traditions of the Irish to younger generations. Theirs was an oral tradition that taught lessons and morals through stories and parables, in much the same way as the Bible. The word druid means 'knower of the oak', reflecting the druid's close connection to nature. The harmony of yin and yang governed their lives. Their gods and goddesses were the Tuatha De Danann who have parallels in many other European pagan religions of the time. Interestingly, most of the religions of the world at this time had numerous gods and goddesses, representing the male and female balance. It was almost unheard of to have a religion or belief system with no female deities.

Around 1000 BC, towards the end of the Bronze Age, the Celts arrived in Ireland. They seem to have populated and spread their culture not by organised force or invasion but by peaceably influencing other peoples through trade connections.[16] Their ideas, gods, technology and way of life seem to have been attractive to other tribes who joined their ranks. This is particularly interesting given that the modern-day European Union, which covers similar territory to the ancient Celtic tribes, seeks to promote similar integration and cross-cultural exchange. Perhaps the Celtic gene is still at work in the corridors of the EU in Brussels. Most historical accounts indicate that the Celts were very impressed by the ways of the druids and they incorporated aspects of their knowledge and wisdom into their own religion and way of life. For the modern reader it is important to point out that our view of religion and spirituality as being independent of science and logic was not the view held by our ancestors. There was no division between their spiritual and physical worlds. The Romans never invaded Ireland thereby allowing the balanced yin and yang culture of the Celts to flourish here.

St Patrick brought Christianity to Ireland during the sixth century. Around this time, many different sects were emerging from the Holy Land; among them was the Church of Rome, the Essenes or Gnostics who were closely linked to Mary Magdalene, and many other splinter groups, all claiming theirs was the one true version of Jesus' message.

St Patrick first arrived in Ireland as a slave, having been kidnapped in either Scotland or Wales; it is from these parts of Britain that his particular sect of Christianity would have originated. I will talk about the Essenes or Gnostics of Egypt and the Cathars of France shortly. Both these groups worshipped the same version of Christianity and it is my belief that the Welsh or Scottish version of Christianity followed by St Patrick originated with the Egyptian Essenes before making its way to the French Cathars and then on to Britain. Why is this important? I will attempt to show you in due course that in the beginning there was a form of Christianity that held the feminine in high regard and worshipped her as Jesus' equal.

At the time of St Patrick, the Christianity of Britain would have been very different to that of Rome. It would have been a blend of Celtic paganism and Christianity, which explains why the Druidic culture of Ireland embraced St Patrick's version of Christianity so readily. Many of the early Irish Christian traditions are also consistent with the Essenes or Gnostic Christians, a sect of Christianity that emerged from Egypt shortly after the crucifixion of Jesus Christ. This is of huge significance, as the Gnostics believed that Mary Magdalene was the bride of Christ and that divinity has both masculine and feminine aspects. The 'lost gospels' or 'Gnostic gospels' which were found at Nag Hammadi in Egypt testify to this. There is some evidence for this Gnostic link in Ireland and there may be more that remains to be discovered. In a County Cork graveyard, scholars found an inscription dating from the fourth century which reads, 'Pray for Olan the Egyptian'.[17] Why an Egyptian would have travelled to Ireland in these times is anyone's guess, but perhaps he could have been a missionary from the Essene tradition. As will become important later, a Celtic princess married the heir to the Merovingian throne, a royal family in the south of France with strong ties to the Gnostics. I believe that this balanced version of Christianity, where both the feminine and the masculine were worshipped, could have travelled from Egypt to the south of France and from there spread to Spain, Italy and Ireland.

There is a good deal of evidence to indicate that Celtic festivals and beliefs were incorporated into this early Irish Celto-Christian Church. In her book *Ever Ancient, Ever New*, Dolores Whelan recites the old Irish proverb, 'God is good and he has a great mother.'[18] This reflects the ancient Irish belief that the balance of all things was essentially yin and yang. This is further reflected by the early Celtic Christian monk who was said to have metaphorically worn two shoes: nature and scripture. Again this demonstrates how even though the belief system was evolving, the sense of balance was being preserved. By now you may be wondering how, if society was really all that wonderful and balanced, so much has changed between then and now.

The early Christians continued to practise this amalgamation of Druidism, paganism and Christianity with great success and balance until Rome heard about it. Christianity in Rome had evolved in line with the masculine and patriarchal style of the Roman Empire, making it very different to Celtic Christianity. The Synod of Whitby was held in AD 664 to bring the British and Irish Christian Church in line with the rules of Rome. This was to mark the beginning of the end of the yin influence in Irish culture and society. You may ask why they didn't stand firm and insist on staying true to their own version of Christianity. In those days, the Roman Church had the power to persecute anyone who did not strictly adhere to its beliefs. During the Inquisition, the Church labelled these people heretics and they were tried and charged before a series of tribunals. There was no shortage of people willing to join the infamous Inquisition and support the eradication of heresy. Whether you were a nobleman or a peasant, if you supported heresy then you risked having your land confiscated and distributed among your inquisitors. It must be understood that the Church of that day was a political and military machine and anything standing in its way was wiped out. As H.J. Massingham says, 'If the British (Celtic) Church had survived, it is possible that the fissure between Christianity and nature, widening through the centuries, would not have cracked the unity of western man's attitude to the universe.'[19]

The Roman Church was one of perhaps three major sects of Christianity which vied for supremacy over the Christian religion. After the death of Jesus many sects claimed to be the true religion. The main groups were the Gnostics who believed the path to God was to be found through gnosis or secret knowledge, the Ebionites who were Jewish Christians and led by James brother of Jesus, and the Pauline Christians whose church was largely based on the works of St Paul. The St Paul Christians were very successful in spreading their message in Rome. Eventually the Roman Empire took on their version of Christianity and so it became the law. This version of Christianity did not share the Gnostics' belief in the divinity of women. This schism of Jesus' followers would cause tragic events to unfold down the line. The early Church of Rome was fanatical about its version of Christianity and was driven as much by politics as spirituality. In AD 325 the Council of Nicaea assembled and declared St Paul's Christianity the official Christian doctrine. The period known as the Dark Ages, which lasted from the fourth to the twelfth century, saw the destruction of anything that challenged the new Church's view of the world, in particular its aversion to the idea of women being admitted to the all-male clerical hierarchy.

In the late eleventh century and early twelfth century, Languedoc in the south of France became a hotbed for a heretical Christian sect known as Catharism. What followed was one of the most intriguing and sensational episodes in the history of the Church. I am of course referring to the quest for the 'holy grail'. *The Da Vinci Code*, Dan Brown's modern retelling of this age-old theme, became one of the best-selling books of all time. Brown's assertion that the feminine has been repressed in the Church resonated with millions of people around the world.

So why is the Cathar heresy so important to the yin and yang balance in the world? The reason is that these people knew a secret so potentially damaging to the Roman Church that its revelation would have brought on a reformation several centuries before anyone had ever even heard of Martin Luther. It is believed that this truth would have brought balance to the yin and yang in western society. So what was it that the Cathars knew?

A good deal of evidence has come to light to suggest that Jesus Christ and many of his followers were from a desert-dwelling spiritual community known as the Essenes. We owe some of our information about these people to the Roman historian Pliny the Elder who wrote about them in some detail, while the discovery of the Dead Sea Scrolls at Qumran in Egypt in 1947 has shed further light. Carbon-dating tests revealed that these scrolls were approximately 2,000 years old and were written around the time of Jesus. We know from these writings that members of the Essenes were allowed to voice their opinions and cast their vote regardless of their sex or rank. As the archaeologist and historian Graham Simmans postulates, 'What seems most likely is that Jesus was brought up in the Essene order, but later in his mission developed a more moderate, tolerant and loving approach.'[20] It appears that the Essenes with who Jesus may have lived were quite puritanical and could be by today's standards described as a monastic people living a simple life of devotion to God.

Simmans based his views on his lifelong study of the Dead Sea Scrolls, the Gnostic Gospels and the Bible, as well as his archaeological digs in Egypt. He sets out a thesis that after the crucifixion, Mary Magdalene, the wife of Jesus, and their child Sarah fled to the south of France to escape persecution. Mary's uncle Joseph of Arimathea, who was a renowned tin merchant, helped them flee. Joseph would have been one of many tin traders operating between the Middle East and Europe, giving him the wherewithal to carry out such a plan. Margaret Starbird, the well-known grail theologian on whose work some of *The Da Vinci Code* was based, supports this same theory.[21] In the book *Holy Blood, Holy Grail*, authors Baigent, Lincoln and Leigh put forward a similar thesis about Mary Magdalene fleeing to the south of France.[22] Having met both Margaret Starbird and Henry Lincoln, they are convinced that the Holy family or Mary Magdalene with Jesus' daughter Tamar (Sarah) made their way to the south of France.

If you travel to Languedoc in the south of France today you will find many place names and churches dedicated to Mary Magdalene. It was here that the Gnostics (Egyptian Jews) sought sanctuary following the crucifixion, bringing with them their traditions and beliefs. Whether it was Mary Magdalene or the Gnostic missionaries who initiated the spread of Catharism, it was soon popular among peasants and nobles alike. The period from the first century to the twelfth century saw many Christians flee what we now know as the Middle East. Alongside these Christians, Muslim traders, Moors, Gauls, Spanish and German tribes all made Languedoc their home. This period in Languedoc was anything but 'dark', with Jews, Christians, Pagans and Muslims all living and trading together harmoniously. The sense of harmony that presided over this diverse community gave rise to a small renaissance. This, combined with the fact that members of the Order of the Knights Templar were based in this region, led to times of great fortune and wealth. The Knights Templar was a military monastic order that served to protect pilgrims travelling from Europe to the Holy Land. The order also played a prominent role in the Crusades from the eleventh to the thirteenth century. As payment for protecting pilgrims travelling to the Holy Land, Rome allowed the knights to lend money and they earned a small fortune from the interest they charged. This was a prosperous time for Languedoc, fuelled by shared knowledge, harmony and the wealth of the Knights Templar.

Central to the Cathars' belief system was the concept of the 'Church of Love' or Amor. With Catharism essentially representing a different version of Catholicism, it is more than just a coincidence that Amor is the reverse spelling of Roma. Another strong theme in Catharism was the belief that the world was dualistic like yin and yang. They believed that the spirit world was good and the material world was evil.[23] The Cathars believed in the rights of all and in the balance of male and female. In fact, many believed that the religion emerged from the doctrine Mary Magdalene brought with her to Languedoc. The Cathars faced the prospect of certain death on grounds of heresy if they claimed that Jesus was married and had a family. So this became the most guarded secret of all time. The holy grail – the family and bloodline of Jesus and Mary.

The Cathars' prosperity soon came to an end. The noble families in the south of France did their best to shelter Catharism from the ever-watchful eye of Rome. The Templars, many being Cathars themselves, also protected the religion along with the *perfecti*, the itinerant preachers of the religion. But the success of the area eventually brought about its downfall. The pope, ironically called Pope Innocent III, feared the erosion of Rome's rule, while King Philip II of France feared the growing power of the south and together they launched an official Inquisition against the Cathars in 1233. There was no shortage of northern nobles willing to join in the Inquisition as they had set their greedy sights on the Cathars' land in the south. Another motivating factor was the fact that many had large outstanding debts, including King Philip, from the war against England. These debts were owed to the Knights Templar and so the Inquisition was seen as an opportunity to eliminate the debts by doing away with the creditors. What followed was a bloody and merciless genocide that saw thousands of innocent people massacred. In Béziers alone, 20,000 men, women and children were put to the sword.[24] When a general asked the papal legate how he would know who was Catholic and who was Cathar, he replied, 'Kill them all. God will recognise his own.'[25] The slaughter continued for ten years. The yang forces of the north destroyed all traces of the balance and harmony that had once prevailed in the south. The final act of this tragic story was played out in 1244 on a mountaintop near the city of Carcassonne at Montségur, which means Mount Secure in English. This fortress, built on a sheer rock outcrop, was a Cathar seminary. When asked to renounce their faith, 150 *perfecti*, knights and their families refused. They were burned at the stake in what is now known as Parc de Pire. Most modern-day visitors to this site report experiencing chilling sensations. The site has become symbolic of the place where the feminine or yin was extinguished.

The following is an extract from the experience of someone I know who visited Montségur. He recounted:

On the way up the stone steps hewn from the raw rock, covered on all sides by high growth and obscured from the eyes of those below, I felt that I was stepping back in time. Not in the sense that one gets of history from an ancient place, but more of one returning home. I had heard of the notion that one may have past lives. For the most part I keep that in the same place as crop circles and UFOs, very interesting but hardly something I would ever have first-hand experience of. Yet climbing these steps, each step was remembering and bringing back a life spent in this place. Climbing higher I got the sense that there were others here. Unseen, silent but there. They were waiting. Waiting as a family or band of brothers does for one of their own to return home. As it was early, the usually crammed path was quiet except for the local guide walking ahead. Sure-footed. Silent. His head covered in a hood giving him the look of a monk or wise one. A true guide. As we ascended in silence, the energy in my feet started to build. Pushing on and up. As we got higher waves of emotion overran me. Indescribable emotions. Ancient emotions. Still higher, we wound our way, the imposing fortress coming into our view at the top of the path. Home at last. Stepping through the weathered and beaten doorway into the exposed heart of the castle, I felt instantly at home. Moreover, the sensations in my body were as if I was in the body of a much larger man, tall, proud, strong, devoted to this place. It was then that I knew I had been and died here. I had burned with my fellow *perfecti* for our faith. The sense of sadness that others had felt here and the pity they felt was not mine. I felt like rejoicing because I was home and because our deaths had been to serve a greater purpose, to create an awareness of what a special place this is and most importantly what it represents. It was at this stage that suddenly a mist surrounded the castle. Here, elevated at the highest point in the surrounding land, the castle sat in the clouds as if floating. Brilliant sunshine bore down and a pervading sense of peace encased that moment. The journey was over after seven hundred years.

It is as though a crucial piece of our history died at Montségur – our link to the Holy Land and to our spiritual heritage. Catharism was driven underground but it survived in code via the remaining Knights Templar and later the Freemasons. But sadly much of the significance of their iconography is lost on modern members of the Freemasons. Today, the suppressed truth of the past is finally coming to light. Books such as *Holy Blood, Holy Grail* and *The Woman with the Alabaster Jar*, together with archaeological finds in the Middle East and France, are providing material to support the fact that Jesus was married and had children. While this may seem like ancient history, it is of huge importance. What would the world be like today if the whole truth had always been known? Would western civilisation have developed differently? Sadly, we will never know the answer to these questions.

What we do know is that massive forces in the form of changing attitudes and a willingness to question the status quo, are currently at work and they are reshaping the society in which we live. The universal law of physics dictates that energy will keep moving until it finds a place of balance. The imbalance in our world is slowly rectifying itself. The West is embracing the spirituality and arts of the East, such as yoga, martial arts, Buddhism, tai chi, qigong, traditional Chinese medicine, Ayurvedic medicine and much more. Meanwhile, if you look to the East you will see a burgeoning industrial revolution similar to that which has already taken place in the West.

The story of the Cathar massacre is just one example of the repeated suppression of the yin throughout history. There is reason to be hopeful, however. With the recent explosion of interest in personal development and spirituality, people are beginning to ask more questions. Religion, governments and society in general are coming under the spotlight. In fact, we are on the cusp of a revolution. We have just experienced a technological revolution that has seen massive advances in areas such as the internet, mobile phones and a myriad of other life-altering technologies. Up next is the spiritual revolution which promises to be even more life- and planet-altering than the technological era. You have only to go as far as your local bookstore to see how rapidly this uprising is approaching. Huge sections of all bookstores are now dominated by what is called 'modern philosophy', 'modern spirituality' and 'personal psychology'. Traditional systems of values and ethics, which were once controlled by the Church and state, are being handed back to the individual. It is you and millions of others like you who are changing today's society and creating the blueprint for the future.

Chapter 7

Yin Yang Health

Your Health is your Wealth

Our health is the cornerstone upon which our happiness rests. To understand our own health, as with all the other aspects we have examined, we must first identify what in our health and healthcare system is yin and what is yang. To help us to understand this, please review the table below:

Yin Medicine (Feminine)	Yang Medicine (Masculine)
Spiritual and Energetic	Mechanical and Chemical
Ancient healing methods	Modern healing methods
The eastern hemisphere	The western hemisphere
Cause focused, why is it happening?	Symptom focused, what is happening?
Holistic view	Specialised focus
Spirit based	Mind based

Looks to the past for cures	Looks to the future for cures
5,000+ years old	350+ years old
Intuition and perception	Logical and systematic
Non hierarchal	Organised hierarchy
Qualitative approach	Quantitative approach

In the western world we need a balance to be brought to the yang western medical profession. We need to balance it not with alternative but with complementary medicine from the East, so that we might avail of the best of both worlds and create a truly balanced healthcare solution. Western medicine is brilliant. It has cured and curbed killer diseases and made our lives vastly more comfortable and happy. It is too easy for people to criticise western medicine for too much reliance on antibiotics, bad management or lack of a patient-first focus and not to take into account the amazing role that it plays in our society. Equally an eastern approach to medicine should also not be written off, since this is an approach that has been evolving for 5,000 years. What I am suggesting is a further development of our western view of medicine from being mind and logic led only to one that includes intuition and a holistic approach. To have a combined style of medicine that treats not just the symptoms but also the underlying emotional, mental or spiritual issue manifesting itself as sickness in the physical body.

In this chapter, I am going to assume that you have a strong grasp and experience of western medicine. Therefore, I am going to concentrate on the yin or the eastern and ancient medicines. Also it is important to note that most of the branches of healing described here are 'complementary' rather than 'alternative'. I know plenty of complementary practitioners who will tell you to take a paracetamol when you might be expecting some wondrous herbal concoction! Complementary medicine is sometimes an alternative or may provide you with an option outside of the western approach, but it is not about one system replacing the other; rather it is about both systems working in harmony.

The greatest challenge to many of you reading this will come from the fact that much of what eastern medicine proposes is that you have created the illness that you suffer. This troubles many people as they may say 'I never asked for cancer'. All of us have loved ones who have died from various diseases and illnesses, and to suggest that they may have been in some part responsible for their own demise may seem insensitive or even offensive. From a western perspective it is easy to take this approach as we do not have a holistic approach to medicine and we look at disease as a misfortune that befalls us rather than something of our own creation. If we hold this belief then we are in danger of not taking responsibility for our own health and wellbeing. Wouldn't it be worth understanding as a cancer patient that there could be a psychological or emotional side to your disease and that by clearing this pattern it would assist in your healing and complement your chemotherapy or radiation treatment?

Most indigenous cultures believed that there was a direct link between the mind, body and soul, and that all these aspects were indivisible. I hear you say 'well what about lifestyle, diet and genetics, surely they affect whether a person gets sick or not?' Yes they do, but here is where the holistic model differs – it looks at all aspects of a person, not just the sickness.

I would like to explore this further with you and introduce you to the work of Dr Deepak Chopra, MD, Brandon Bays, Kathleen Milner, Caroline Myss, Dr C. Norman Shelly, MD, Louise Hay and many other complementary medicine pioneers.[26] They are generally in agreement that physical pain and disease is caused by something called cell memories. This is also known as psychosomatic medicine – i.e. the thoughts or emotions that you are experiencing manifest, especially the negative ones, as injury, pain, disease and sickness. An example of how this could affect a person's health would be two brothers who had an inherited heart defect, giving them both an increased chance of having a heart attack. One is very negative and expects the worst in life and sure enough suffers a heart attack. The other brother with a positive outlook does not have a heart attack. In this instance the heart attack could be attributed to the emotional toxicity that the negative brother carried.

Louise Hay, in her wonderful book *You Can Heal Your Body*, lists the emotional causes of ailments. In her own case, using positive affirmations and nutrition, she cured herself of cervical cancer in six months.[27] She realised that having been raped at the age of five she had stored negative cellular memories in that part of her body. Using her own philosophy of loving your body and using positive affirmations she not only healed herself but has also helped thousands of others. Her message resonates with so many people that her book has sold over 35 million copies and has been translated into thirty-seven languages. Another pioneer, Brandon Bays, healed herself of a football-sized tumour in six and a half weeks using natural methods.[28] These are real and documented cases of terminal illnesses being cured because the people suffering them took responsibility for the illness and thereby also took responsibility for healing themselves.

On the subject of genetics, the propensity for illness can pass on not just in DNA but also in behavioural patterns. We know from the work of Dr Deepak Chopra that cellular disease can be created by negative emotions, beliefs and thoughts – 'the biochemistry of the body is a product of awareness. Belief, thoughts and emotions create the chemical reactions that uphold life in every cell. An ageing cell is the end product of awareness that has forgotten how to remain new.'[29] Taking this insight and knowing that behavioural patterns are passed on from parent to child, we could conclude that it may be possible for the negative thought patterns to pass through generations and have a similar effect on the cells of successive generations. Breast cancer in women is sometimes linked to issues regarding mothering. These could be over-mothering or carrying constant fear and worry for your children or not ever feeling that you were properly loved by your mother. Many complementary practitioners would agree that this could result in breast cancer forming as this is the area of the body where that emotional pattern attacks. It is not the only reason for breast cancer, but if it plays any part at all isn't it worth correcting the emotional pattern? Now take the scenario of a daughter who has a mother that always worried about her, then has a child of her own. She will have learned that the natural state for a mother to be in is a state of worry over her child. In turn her daughter has a child and again the mother is a worrier. As you can see, behavioural traits that are learned can pass from generation to generation. It is thought that this is why we can sometimes see the same illness running in successive generations. I am totally prepared to accept that this could be coded into the DNA; however, I do not think we can rule out the possibility that psychosomatic conditions could run in families as successive generations pass on negative belief systems and thinking, leading to a damaging effect on the health of individuals.

So what else can we learn from the ancients and the yin or eastern approach? For me the most striking discovery in medicine is redefining the concept of what causes illness and sickness. Healing today under the guise of western medicine treats the symptom but sometimes fails to tackle all the underlying causes. As the Chinese would say in regard to treating symptoms and not causes 'you kill the messenger'. In this they mean that each pain, itch, irritation, injury or disease that we get is a sign that something is out of balance. This is not to say that we shouldn't treat the symptoms, but we should ask the question why are the symptoms there? For example lower back pain is commonly linked in psychosomatic medicine to financial worry. If you are suffering lower back pain now or have in the past, ask yourself the question: am I worried about my finances? Am I worried about debt? Am I worried about having enough?

Traditional Chinese medicine, Reiki and affirmation healing such as that extolled by Louise Hay work on the assumption that injury and not just illness can result from carrying negative emotional patterns. The injury can be caused as the propensity exists for the injury because of the emotional pattern carried. This is why two people suffering the same accident could have different injuries. It all depends where the weakness exists. The left side of the body is feminine yin and relates to our own sense of the feminine and it is also where we will be affected by trauma in our life caused by our reactions to mothers, sisters, wives etc. The right represents our masculine yang and relates to relationships with fathers, brothers, husbands etc.

The left knee in some branches of healing is related to letting go of the mother. The right knee is related to letting go of the father. I know two brothers who, having lost their mother very suddenly, both suffered left knee injuries while playing football. As a life and business coach I could tell that both of them have never really dealt with her death. While they refuse to let her go they will continue to have pain and problems with their left knees. Have you ever suffered knee injuries? If so think about the relationship that you had with your parents at that time. Or did one of them pass away and then you received an injury?

Our bodies are like signposts. They act as a canvas for the emotional and mental states we carry. As we often ignore or are unaware of both these states, we require the messages of the body to help us to identify where to work on releasing negative emotions and thoughts. We get signals or signs from our bodies to let us know that on some level we are ill at ease. It could be a thought, a memory or an emotion that we are holding that is causing the pain.

Stress most simply demonstrates the link between our feelings and our physical health. What happens to you when you get really stressed? Firstly, you will be projecting yourself into the future, imagining an event that has not happened and may never happen. Even so you persist in building up fear about this future event. It may be attaining the month sales targets. It may be your children going to school. It may be worrying about finances. Whatever it is you will find it creates a physical symptom. It may be a rash, an itch, a sore neck, back pain, heavy sore eyes, headaches, dry mouth, cramp, belly ache, irritable bowl syndrome or one of many other such signs. Most of us just reach for the cure, the tablet, the drug. What we are doing is killing the messenger.

Instead of killing the messenger what if we decided to listen? To pay attention to our body and to understand its language. If we do this we can achieve the key to our psychology. Just as body language allows you to read another person, your physical state gives you the true measure of your emotional and mental state. The yang always rushes in to fix everything, to find the solution, the panacea that cures all ills. The yin on the other hand is reflective, taking in and processing the problem at hand, allowing the answer to arise naturally from awareness. Each one of us has this ability locked inside us. Each one of us has the ability to have better health, by paying attention to the signs inside us. If we can unite our yang western knowledge of healing with our yin knowledge, we have great power at our hands that can heal through both logic and intuition.

So how do we start to listen to our bodies? What can we do to decipher the complex signals they give us? Well for a start we can look at our patterns. I know people that every year will have a dose of the flu at Christmas time. I know a woman that every autumn gets a bad infection in her back which requires hospital treatment. What is it at these times that is causing the problem? I know the people in both those situations will blame it on bad luck and think no more of it. But what would they hear if they listened to their bodies? In both those cases the messenger is the sickness and injury, but the real culprit is their thought patterns, lifestyle and the stress in their lives.

Cancer is a huge killer today and a puzzle that science tries to manage, but has very little idea how it is caused. We know from research that Dr Deepak Chopra has accessed that, with the exception of the brain cells, almost every cell in your body is renewed and replaced every six months. 'You make a new liver every six weeks, a new skeleton once every three months, a new stomach lining every five days, a new skin once a month.'[30] If this is the case then why can somebody have cancer for ten years? What is it that makes those cells reproduce in a malignant form? Western or yang medicine will claim that it is a cell abnormality or DNA that reproduces and spreads as a tumour and they are right, but WHY is the abnormality reproducing when the cell reproduces? Eastern or yin medicine will look at the individual and assess what is out of balance in their lives and what is causing the continuation of the disease. This is where we go back to cell memories.

Every cell in our bodies is 90 per cent water. Water can carry an emotional charge. Dr Masuro Emoto in his book *Hidden Messages in Water* shows incredible images of frozen water crystals. What is interesting is how the water has been treated. All the water is bottled and a typed label is placed on each bottle. Some labels say love, others hate, others friendship and so on. The bottles are left for some time to 'absorb' the word written on it. Fascinatingly, when the water is viewed under a microscope and photographed with a high speed camera, in the bottles with the positive words the most beautiful symmetrical and spectacular crystal shapes can be seen. In contrast, in the bottles with the negative words there are shapeless, deformed, unattractive shapes. The difference is striking. Taking the experiment further Dr Emoto exposed bottles of water to music; some to classical pieces like Bach and Beethoven and others to heavy metal and death metal. As you can guess the classical pieces form beautiful crystals while the heavy metal forms deformed, cracked and broken ones. The same results were obtained with clear spring water revealing beautiful and colourful formations and polluted water resulting in incomplete, asymmetric patterns with dull colours.[31] Now imagine what happens to the 90 per cent water in your cells every time you have a negative thought or emotion. It's not pretty is it? Now take guilt, self pity, anger, hatred, worry, stress or the myriad of other poisonous emotions that we have regularly and you can see why some symptoms never leave us.

The only way to be free is to release these suppressed emotions, these negative thought patterns and replace them with positivity. This coupled with modern western medicine makes a powerful alliance. I know that the sceptics among you will say that this 'mind over matter' mumbo jumbo doesn't work, just because you think positivity won't make you live any longer. You may be right, maybe you won't live any longer, but you will be happier and healthier while you are here. What is proven is the human body's ability to do incredible things when the power of the mind is harnessed. India and Tibet are full of holy men who have spent their life meditating and have harnessed the full powers of the body. Indian gurus have been observed in laboratory conditions to have not taken water or food for weeks. Professor Herbert Benson of Harvard Medical School observed and documented three Buddhist monks practising Tum-Mo meditation. Each monk had three wet and freezing cold sheets placed one after the other on their bare upper bodies. After about an hour each sheet was dry and steam was seen to be rising off the monks. As the first sheet became dry, the next was placed on the monks. After three sheets were dried by each monk, it could be concluded that these monks through meditation could completely change their metabolism and the functions of the human body.[32] This is yin and yang in balance. Professor Herbert also noted the monks could create up to fifteen degrees more heat from their hands than the rest of their body.

What is certain is that we are only at the tip of understanding what the human body is capable of doing. Sara Lazar, also from Harvard Medical School, has documented that regular meditation increases the size of the brain, in particular 'cognitive and emotional processing and well-being'.[33] When we look at eastern medicine we find a recurring theme of balancing energy systems. What we require in the West is an appreciation of this and if it resonates with us, to embrace it as part of our healthcare.

I believe that an important understanding of ourselves can come from an understanding of our energy system. We are all electrical beings. The Chinese call this 'chi', the Indians call it 'prana', while we call it energy. It simply means life-force. It is the difference between a corpse and a living person. We experience our own electrical field every day but are largely unaware of it. Electrical impulses are the messengers that fire along our nervous system. Our brains are a hive of electrical activity. In fact there is a type of photography that can capture the energy field around us. Called Kirlian photography, by connecting to the object or person the camera can catch the electrical field emitted. Another type of photography using fibre optics can be used to photograph a person's aura. Our aura is the field of light or vibration that surrounds us. All light and sound are frequencies and the frequencies we can see with the naked eye are red, orange, yellow, green, blue, indigo and violet. They are what is known as the spectrum of white light. Outside the spectrum are x-ray, infra-red etc. Our aura is made up of light that most cannot see without training. A person's aura can give a clue as to their health. For example if a person had liver damage this might show up as blackness or darkness in the aura. Healthy auras show up as vibrant strong colours.

Most of the eastern peoples, particularly in India, have a strong understanding of this system. The Sanskrit word for the energy centres that we all possess is chakra. We have seven main chakras listed below:

Name	Location	Colour	Age*	Purpose
Root	Base of spine	Red	0-7	Survival, connection to the earth, abundance
Sacral	Lower abdomen	Orange	7-14	Relationships, sexuality, passion, drive
Solar	Solar Plexus	Yellow	14-21	Emotions, self-control, inner guidance

Heart	Centre of chest	Green/ Pink	21-28	Love, self esteem, the centre
Throat	Neck	Blue	28-35	Truth, creativity, highest communication
Brow	Forehead	Indigo	*	Insight, intuition, understanding
Crown	Top of head	Violet	*	Enlightenment, spiritual connection

* Age refers to the age that each chakra comes into its full strength. The Brow and Crown chakra represent higher spiritual functions and are not linked to age. They can be present from birth depending on how evolved the spirit is. The chakra system is connected to a belief in reincarnation.

These chakras are an energy system that work together in a way similar to the way that our physical organs work together. Each supports the other and they pass energy between them. Chakras for all purposes look like vortexes as described by Barbara Ann Brennan, an ex-NASA research scientist who is now a healer.[34] Each chakra has two sides. One that takes in and one that sends out. For example, the solar plexus chakra is located at our stomach and lower back, the throat chakra at the front and back of our neck. The seven on the back bring energy inward (yin) and the seven on the front send energy outwards (yang). Have you ever noticed that some people completely drain your energy? What they are doing is pulling energy from your chakras to feed their own. Negative situations also affect our chakras. If we work or live in negative surroundings then these chakras can start to close. For example, if our heart chakra at our back closes then our ability to take in love (yin) will be compromised. On the other hand if our heart chakra on the front closes then we will be unable to give love (yang). All the chakras need to take in as well as give out for us to feel healthy. When we block our chakras with negativity, bad diet and lack of exercise then eventually we will start to experience a physical symptom near to that chakra. So in the case of the heart this may mean anything from heartburn to a heart attack if the chakras are fully closed.

The chakra system may seem very far removed from western medicine, but surprisingly it is not. Using our yang-based logic and reason, we can see that every chakra is actually located anatomically beside the hormone secreting endocrine glands which are part of the lymphatic system. This system is used to remove toxins and transport hormones around the body. The brow chakra is connected to the pineal gland, the heart to the thymus, the solar plexus chakra to the adrenal glands, the ovaries and testes to the sacral chakra and so on. When we overlay this medical knowledge with the chakra system we suddenly see that huge similarities appear.[35]

Reiki and other healing methods work to balance these chakras so that energy flows easily and creates health at an etheric level or spirit level. Knowing about the link to the endocrine glands, one of the reactions to balancing of the chakras is for the related glands to release hormones that make us feel better and therefore leads to healing. As a Reiki master I have felt the energy flowing from my hands to the chakra of the person I am working on and have also experienced it on the receiving end. In Reiki we believe that this energy is chi, prana or universal energy and that as a practitioner we are simply channelling energy to help a person heal. The energy does not come from the practitioner; rather the Reiki healer acts like a conduit for the energy that is already there. The ancient people of India and China, as well as many modern-day experts like Caroline Myss and Barbaran Ann Brennan, believe that health issues can start first in our aura or energetic field. They then transfer to our emotional systems and then finally manifest after time in our physical body. The logic then suggests that if we can keep our energetic field healthy, we keep our emotional well-being and physical bodies healthy.

What we must constantly do is to look at ourselves in terms of both yin and yang. One of my clients who is an accountant and was very yang-based in his thinking, started to do some coaching sessions and Reiki work with me. His mother had died suddenly a few years earlier and in his opinion western medicine had failed to save her. After several months of very strong headaches he spoke to his doctor who advised him to have a precautionary brain scan. He refused, saying that he would only trust alternative or complementary medicine. He shared this story with me proudly as if seeking my approval for his choice. He was surprised when I advised him that he should in fact have the scan, but also have a few acupuncture and Reiki sessions to relieve the mental pressure in his head. As western medicine cannot be called a panacea to all ills, neither can alternative or spiritual healing. While most in the western world can be yang-minded, we can also become too yin-minded. The key is to take the best of both aspects of medicine and find our balance for health.

As mentioned earlier, every cell in our bodies is mostly water. Taking this a step forward, physicists know that all these cells are made of atoms. These atoms are 99.9999 per cent empty. That is to say there is nothing in this space that science can measure. Therefore are we 99.9999 per cent nothing? The yin wisdom or ancient way of thinking would correspond with the physicists view that we are 99.9999 per cent empty space and say yes, in the fact that there is in the atoms a percentage of no matter or anti-matter as science will call it. The ancients believed that this anti-matter was in fact energy. A type of energy that reveals itself as pure potential or the divinity that is in every living thing. This is where the prana, chi, life-force or pure potential resides. It is the stuff that creates galaxies and creates us. The ancient peoples understood this and based their healing and medicine on the fact that for true health the body but also the mind, emotion and spirit needed to be nurtured and cared for. All the ancient cultures of the world make some reference to this type of energy, from the Egyptians to the Celts. Our modern minds, conditioned by the yang society we live in, find this concept of energy very difficult to grasp. You must understand you are an electrical being. If you don't believe me think about the last time you got a static shock. Your car or someone else transmitted this energy to you which you felt. It is crucial to understand the concept of energy so that we can bring a yin balance to our yang understanding.

There is a new enlightened form of medicine combining western yang logic and eastern yin intuition that can see us transcend many illnesses and diseases. What is required is a resurrection of the understanding of the ancient ways of medicine in combination with the wonders of science. We need to connect to the ways that have been suppressed: the old ways of the druids, medicine men, witch doctors, high priests and priestesses. The battle of the early religions for supremacy saw the torture and burning of thousands, particularly women who were classed as witches. Most were no more than herbalists who used knowledge of flora and fauna passed on for generations to heal the sick. In the East where these struggles did not cast their long shadow, much of this knowledge survived. It is up to each one of us to take responsibility for our own health and to educate ourselves not just about the modern miracles of science, but also the rich legacy of health-based knowledge that our ancestors have left us. Many western doctors now send people for acupuncture and many healthcare professionals are learning and studying the alternative and complementary fields. A combination of yin and yang working in harmony together would be the working relationship that Caroline Myss has with Dr Norman Shelly. Myss is a medical intuitive, in that she can psychically 'tune' into the body of a patient and see a tumour or disease, and can also receive guidance on how to heal the ailment. Shelly is a neurosurgeon and would blind test Myss just by giving her the name and age of the patient he was treating. Myss would then tune in to the patient, possibly picking up other ailments or information about the condition that could help the recovery of the patient. Together they represent yin and yang the balance of ancient methods with new. Myss has worked with up to fifteen physicians in the US.[36]

The massive growth in yoga, homeopathy, amatsu, acupuncture, Reiki, tai chi, TCM, Auyrevedic medicine and many other philosophies and methods bear testament to the spread of this knowledge concerning health. My challenge to you is to put aside preconceived notions and belief systems that family, religion and society may have handed you. Find out for yourself. Have a session of acupuncture, go feel the magical healing qualities of Reiki, explore the relaxation and inner calm of tai chi, develop suppleness, discipline, strength and the calm of the inner yin through yoga. If, after your own investigations, you feel you have achieved nothing, then walk away with the knowledge that your preconceived notions were right! What though, if, like Galileo, you experience something you cannot deny? Then you will have left the thinking of pure yang and entered the realm of thinking of yin and yang in balance.

EXERCISE

There are so many techniques, tools and practices that you could engage in either to heal a condition or maintain good health. In my research and experience all healing systems from a yin perspective come down to two things: releasing fear and bringing in love. For thousands of years people have chanted. Today we call them mantras, mottos and prayers. They all work in the same way, by creating positive vibrations that heal.

I would like you to do just one thing – say the following mantra twenty-one times when you wake up and before you go to sleep. Do this for seven days. When you say it place your hands on your heart:

I love myself, I release all fear

Notice how you feel after saying this. Some will feel elated, some teary or emotional, some peaceful. If you have a particular ailment place you hands on the area that is affected while saying the mantra or affirmation. After seven days your energy field will be clearer and you will feel a difference.

Chapter 8

The Yin Yang Environment

REAPING WHAT WE SOW

We need only look to our environment to see the large-scale impact of a society driven by yang rather than yin. We live in what is naturally the most finely balanced world imaginable. Millions of factors have combined to produce the right circumstances for life to exist and it is only when you stack up all of these factors that you realise just how lucky we are to be here. Yet on a day-to-day basis we tamper with this balance and cause irrevocable damage to the world we live in.

One theory behind the earth's origins is that our planet once had a twin and billions of years ago it collided with this planet, resulting in a massive crash that pushed us into our present orbit. This crash loosened billions of tons of rocks which sped into space and over time coalesced to form the moon. The moon controls the earth's tides and helps ocean currents to circulate, which in turn creates our weather systems and enables our planet to function. The next important factor in the development of life on earth is our distance from the sun. If we were any closer we would burn up in the blistering heat, like the planet Venus, but if we were any further away we would be freezing like Mars. We are perfectly located for water to form and organic life to function.

The shooting stars that often light up the night sky give us some clue as to the billions of tons of meteoroids that are hurtling around the solar system. These meteors are very dangerous and if they collide with the earth the results could be catastrophic. Millions of years ago, one of these massive meteors hit the earth and gave rise to the Ice Age that wiped out the dinosaurs. The power of this meteor has been compared to the detonation of one million atomic bombs similar to that which was dropped on Hiroshima during the Second World War.[37] Were it not for the protective presence of Jupiter these missiles would hit us regularly. Jupiter is approximately 300 times greater in mass and 1,000 times greater in volume than the earth, giving it a massive field of gravity that pulls these huge meteors towards it and away from the fragile earth. Meanwhile, the sun, a very unusual slow-burning star, gives the earth just enough light, heat and energy to function. Already, you can see why scientists believe there is such a remote chance of finding earth-like life anywhere else in the universe.

The unique balance of cosmic forces that allows life to exist on earth is repeated on a smaller scale in our ecosystems and environment. We can see how even the slightest change in our ecosystem or food chain can have a knock-on effect with disastrous consequences. For example, popular seaside holiday destinations worldwide are suffering jellyfish invasions as numbers of the gelatinous creatures reach plague proportions. Scientists blame man's effect on decreasing the numbers of sea turtles as a major cause. 'All seven species of sea turtles eat jellyfish and all seven species are endangered. Their survival is threatened by fishing lines that trap them, pollution, beach development, climate change and sales of turtles and turtle parts,' says The National Science Federation, an independent US federal agency.[38]

Nature is the most perfect example of yin yang balance. The law of balance is the law of nature and humans are kidding themselves if they think they are not governed by these same rules. We evolved from nature and depend upon it for our continued existence. While we may believe that through science we have triumphed over the laws of nature, the cost of this triumph is slowly becoming apparent. We are not balancing the yang activity of constant harvesting with the yin activity of sowing and this is slowly killing both us and our planet. The yang practice of drilling for oil is proving equally costly. This natural resource has fuelled the industrial world but at a huge cost to our environment. Whenever we burn fossil fuels such as oil, the gas carbon dioxide (CO_2) is emitted into the atmosphere. Over time this gas causes the planet to overheat. This is more commonly known as the greenhouse effect.

Carbon dioxide is a naturally occurring gas. In safe quantities it acts as an insulator, trapping the sun's warmth and preventing the planet from freezing. In nature, the trees and plants need to absorb CO_2 for photosynthesis to take place. However, by burning and clearing forests we are increasing the levels of CO_2 in our atmosphere which is in turn compounding the overheating of the planet. All of these factors have a domino effect. As the planet continues to overheat areas of permafrost (ground that is permanently frozen) in the northern and southernmost reaches of our planet are melting, in turn releasing further massive amounts of CO_2. This CO_2 is a natural by-product of rotting vegetation that, up until now, had been contained in the frozen ground. Increasing temperatures will continue to melt the polar ice shelf which will in turn cause rising flood levels that will make countless people homeless. Changing weather patterns will lead to droughts and crop failures and fierce storms and tsunamis will become more frequent. In essence, the earth is trying to restore balance by taking away our ability to live on this planet.

Food shortages are becoming an increasing problem around the world. Land that was previously used to grow food is now being devoted to bio-fuel crops such as rapeseed and sugar beet. Ironically, CO_2 emissions are soaring because rainforests are being cleared away to make room for these so-called environmentally friendly fuel crops. Our food is running out fast. In 2006 the EU found that during five of the previous six years it had consumed more grain than it had produced. We are at our lowest level of grain reserves in thirty-four years.[39] This demonstrates a lack of global thinking and understanding of the most fundamental laws of nature. The yang need for bigger cars and the industrial appetite for oil will inevitably lead to even worse food shortages down the line. The implication for society is huge. In 2004 *The Times* reported that MI5, the British Internal Security Service, assesses the threat to national security on a 'four-meal basis'.[40] In other words, they believe that within forty-eight hours of running out of food and watching their children go hungry, people will take the law into their own hands. They will do whatever it takes to protect themselves and their families. We are only ever a few meals away from anarchy. MI5 calculate the fallout from terrorist attacks by the effect on food, transport, electricity, gas and so on. Think about it. What would you do to feed your children if they had not eaten in days? Such questions will haunt us as long as we allow the yang to dominate our society.

The imbalance between the First World and the Third World's use of the earth's resources is also leading towards a frightening conflict. In the battle for precious resources, lives become cheap. In a 2007 briefing to the US Senate, Lester Brown of the earth Policy Institute summed up this disparity when he spoke about the conversion of grain into ethanol to power cars. He declared, 'The stage is now set for direct competition for grain between the eight hundred million people who own automobiles, and the world's two billion poorest people.'[41]

This imbalance is not just a modern phenomenon. As early as the eighteenth century, the British political economist Robert Thomas Malthus predicted, 'The power of population is so superior to the power of the earth to produce subsistence for man, that premature death must in some shape or other visit the human race.' Malthus would probably have been shocked if he had learned that although it took 10,000 years for the world to amass a global population of 2 billion, in our lifetimes we will see the world's population rise from 6.7 billion in January 2009 to an estimated 9 billion by 2042.[42] With the EU directive that up to 10 per cent of fuel for transport be bio-fuel by 2010 and the fact that much of future agriculture is to be devoted to bio-fuels instead of food, we may very well see Malthus' predictions materialise.[43]

As nations like China and India become increasingly industrialised, the world needs more resources than ever before. This vicious circle intensifies when we see developed countries such as Britain and the US invading Iraq to access the region's oil reserves because, as we have seen, fuel shortages could be detrimental to the fabric of their societies. It is poignant that as I write this, snow has fallen on Iraq for the first time in living memory, providing a clear indication of the effects of global warming on a country that lies at the epicentre of the energy war.

Staying with food we can see how a by-product of genetic engineering and massive-scale intensive farming has led our food to need lots of fertilisers and organophosphates and other chemicals to stave off disease. Much of this is due to the forced growing of crops. Petrochemical fertilisers are used to create faster and heavier harvest yields. The net effect is that we have bigger and more beautiful-looking produce, but it is laced with ill-health-linked chemicals not found on organic produce. While government research in the UK claims that there is no difference between organic and non-organic vegetables, the Soil Association in the UK quoted in the *Guardian* claim: 'There is now a rapidly growing body of evidence which shows significant differences between the nutritional composition of organic and non-organic food. Studies have shown that on average organic food has higher levels of iron, calcium, magnesium, phosphorus and vitamin C.'[44]

The main difference between organic and non-organic food seems to be freshness. We are obviously going to eat food from our back garden when it is much fresher than food that is grown in some far-off country and then imported. So the less fresh food is, the lower its nutritional value, because the longer vegetables are out of the ground the more they lose essential vitamin and minerals. Why do you think so many products are now fortified with vitamins and iron? Another reason is that the crops can no longer absorb these minerals from the ground as they used to, because they are now forced to grow quickly to fulfil commercial demands. As we are all aware, a balanced diet of fruit and vegetables is essential for our physical well-being. But long journey times from the farm to the consumer mean that many fruit and vegetables are now being irradiated to make them last longer. Irradiation has been shown to remove up to 50 per cent of some vitamins in the food.[15] Thankfully, since 2007, legislation has been introduced that will require companies in the EU and US to declare on the packaging if the food has been irradiated.

The large distances from the source of our food has also affected the manufacturing of foods for the worse. Owing to the fact that food may perish over long journeys many food producers add hydrogenated fats to counter this. Most nutritionists agree that hydrogenated fats are a major source of ill health, high cholesterol and obesity, as our bodies cannot break down these fats, artificially created from natural fats such as corn oil. They are highly heated and this makes them very stable at room temperature. So why are they used if our bodies struggle to process them? Quite simply they extend the shelf life of products, allowing the producer and retailer a greater profit. The flawed relationship between our agricultural policy, food production and our health is plain to see. The imbalance between the two is directly affecting our health.

We have lost touch with our yin sides and this has cost us dearly. Take the tsunami that killed thousands of people when it hit the coasts of several countries in the Indian Ocean on 26 December 2004. In the hours leading up to this tragedy, holidaymakers and locals alike watched domestic and wild animals go berserk all around them as they rushed inland in search of higher ground. Meanwhile, on seeing the sea recede down the beach many perplexed humans actually walked out after the tide, some carrying cameras to record the scene. It is well documented that animals have a sixth sense when it comes to disasters and that they are often the first warning signs we have. But the people in these coastal regions were out of touch with the natural world and their yin sides and, unlike their ancestors who would have sensed the seriousness of the animals fleeing, they did not react to the strange phenomena preceding the tsunami. Humans have the same intuition and inbuilt ability to avert danger as animals, but sadly most of us are so out of touch with nature that we no longer understand the rules that govern it.

Isaac Newton's Third Law of Motion states that for every action there is an equal and opposite reaction. From the time the dinosaurs roamed the earth through to the present day, we have had a much greater impact on our planet than any other inhabitants. The dinosaurs were wiped out by a natural catastrophe but mankind seems to be in the process of co-authoring its own extinction. The laws of nature demands balance. If we do not respect this then the earth will eventually become inhospitable to human life. As Al Gore remarked in his Academy Award-winning documentary *An Inconvenient Truth*, 'the battle is not for the survival of the planet but the survival of mankind'. The earth has been subjected to millions of events that have altered its shape and environment, yet billions of years later it is still here. Thousands of years from now, or even hundreds of years, will people be able to say the same?

In 1936, shortly before the Second World War, Winston Churchill remarked that 'we are entering a period of consequences'. The world as we knew it was about to change. This sentiment was echoed in August 2005 when Hurricane Katrina swept across the southern states of America, leaving a trail of destruction and human misery in its wake. In the past, hurricanes such as Katrina would normally have blown out over the Gulf of Mexico, causing minimal damage. However, the warmer sea temperatures caused by global warming intensified the storm and Katrina became one of the costliest and deadliest storms in American history. Such hurricanes are just the beginning of this new age of environmental uncertainty.

Forty per cent of the world's drinking water comes from the Himalayas, but with the annual snowfall there declining as a result of global warming people could soon be facing an acute water shortage. In the Antarctica and the North Pole, the melting ice shelves threaten to raise global sea levels by up to twenty feet, submerging the homes of millions of people living in coastal towns and cities. Imagine the chaos that would ensue if all these people were made homeless. Another frightening aspect of the polar ice caps melting is that they currently balance the heat of the equator. This heat differential powers the world's ocean currents and weather systems as heat is shuffled from the equator to the poles. If the melting ice caps cause a massive release of cold fresh water into the North Atlantic this could shut down the North Atlantic Drift, the current that keeps Europe warm. If this happens we could be facing another Ice Age similar to that which occurred during the Palaeolithic period when a massive body of frozen water in Canada spilled into the North Atlantic.

So is it too late? Have we got a snowball's chance in hell of living through this? Thankfully, the answer is yes. We have already managed to avert a major environmental disaster – the hole in the ozone layer. The global banning of CFC gases addressed this issue and the ozone layer is now slowly returning to normal. We can make a difference if we decide to take action.[46]

I believe that part of the reason we are destroying the planet is that we have lost our own sense of balance and can no longer recognise or appreciate the balance required in the world around us. Our ancestors had a better understanding of the need to take care of the world. Mother earth, as the American Indians called her, provided for her children only if balance was maintained. The Indians therefore only ever killed enough animals to satisfy their needs and always gave thanks to the animal for sustaining them. Our Celtic ancestors were also very in tune with nature. They divided the year into two major phases. The *giamos* time related to winter, darkness, the realm of the goddess and the feminine spirit. Its balance was *samos* time which related to summer, light, the realm of the god and the masculine spirit. The summer and winter solstices were major festivals as were the spring and autumn equinoxes. Their lives, work, families, religion and laws all revolved around the Celtic calendar. Many of these Celtic festivals were absorbed into the modern Christian Church and are still celebrated in countries all over the world. The winter solstice is now Christmas, the spring equinox or *ester* is now Easter, the summer solstice is mid-summer celebrations and the autumn equinox is now the harvest festival of Halloween.

It is up to each one of us to drive a change in attitudes and practices and bring the planet back into balance. Both collectively and individually we need to take responsibility for restoring balance. This doesn't mean you have to begin by trying to prevent the clearing of rainforests in Borneo or by preserving the habitat of Arctic polar bears. The first change we need to make is within ourselves. It is easy to blame the politicians and criticise them for inaction. But remember you put them there. The next time a politician or a member of his party seeks your vote, raise the green issue and urge them to take action. One of the politician's main interests is securing his next term, so if you and enough others make saving the planet your issue then the politician will take it on board as their potential ticket to re-election. Another small step you can take is to reduce your carbon footprint – the amount of carbon you, as an individual, contribute to the atmosphere either directly or indirectly. The average American generates 7.5 tons of carbon per year.[47] It is possible for us all to become carbon neutral. We can offset our carbon output through such practices as planting trees, using energy-efficient appliances and using naturally generated energy. For more information and advice on saving the planet, visit the www.climatecrisis.net website.

We need to take action now, if not for ourselves then for our children and the future generations who will inherit our planet. It will require a lot of work if we are to keep 'green' on the agenda. We can see this in the case of the whaling protests in Japan during the 1990s. Despite the fact that 70 per cent of the Japanese public were against whaling, once the initial protests died down the whaling fleet resumed hunting and killing humpback whales. These so-called 'scientific' missions are fuelled by the yang-based thinking of rich people who want to eat whale meat. The missions are classed as scientific to circumvent an internationally signed and recognised treaty banning the hunting and killing of whales except for scientific purposes. Another example of these self-motivated yang-based groups could be seen during George Bush's term as the president of America. Lobby groups from the mining and oil industry actively petitioned Bush to open up areas of preservation in Alaska, one of America's last unspoilt wildernesses. This would have caused untold damage to the area and would have further compounded the crisis caused by fossil fuels. These examples show how our planet is constantly under attack from these yang-based groups who simply want their way at any cost. We must be vigilant and try to ensure that our own approach is always a balance of yin and yang; an approach that balances our need to take from the earth with a commitment to also give back. We are all connected to nature whether we realise it or not. If we stand still for a moment and try to become more aware of nature, our dormant yin connection will rise up in us again. The future of our planet and of the human race demands that we restore a sense of balance to nature by bringing yin back in line with yang.

Five Practical Steps for Saving the Planet

1. Plant a tree. It will absorb an average of one ton of carbon during its lifetime.

2. Don't leave electrical appliances on standby. This can save up to 30 per cent energy use.

3. Drive with your tyres fully pumped and you will be 3 per cent more efficient.

4. Walk, cycle or use public transport. Every mile you don't drive saves 500gms of CO_2.

5. Replace a regular light bulb with an energy-saver bulb and save 68kgs of CO_2 each year.[48]

Chapter 9

Yin Yang Spirituality

FINDING THE DIVINE FEMININE

The mere mention of the word spirituality is enough to send some people running for cover. I believe the reason for this stems from the fact that our society sees religion and spirituality as one and the same, when in fact they are very different. Religion is defined by a dogma or a set way of doing, thinking and interpreting. Religion can be flawed if, for example, it believes that its way is the only way and that all others are wrong. When we think of spirituality, or confuse the word with religion, we are potentially writing off our spirit, the very core of our being.

Let us look first at the subject of religion: the good, the bad and the ugly. Many of us are very aware of the baggage that certain religions carry. We may even hold religion responsible for a great deal of conflict and strife in the world. Who could blame us for thinking this when we see the atrocities and wars that have been carried out in the name of faith since the beginning of time? In Northern Ireland, after decades of conflict, the warring Catholic and Protestant factions have finally put aside their differences to work towards a better future. Looking back, it is clear that religion was not the sole problem at the heart of the conflict; rather it served as an identifier. There were no theologians in the background outlining why the other religion should be suppressed. Instead the clergy on both sides focused on finding an end to the violence and hurt. The following joke perfectly encapsulates this theory. A Dublin man was visiting a Belfast city bar during the Troubles in the 1970s. He was minding his own business when a group of rough-looking people approached him. They asked him straight out, 'Are you a Protestant or a Catholic?' The Dublin man replied that he was neither, that he was in fact Jewish. Expecting this to be the end of the matter he was surprised when they pressed him further. 'Are you a Protestant or Catholic Jew?' they asked. This joke shows that religion was just a tribal identifier; the real source of conflict stemmed from issues of equality, autonomy and freedom from discrimination.

We can all readily list countless religious wars, from the Crusades and the Inquisition to the present-day Arab/Israeli, or Muslim/Jewish, conflict. Such conflicts give religion a bad name. But every religion has its extremists who detract from the overall goodness they generally contain. People are turning away from religion en masse for reasons such as the revelation of sexual abuse scandals in the Catholic Church or the violent extremism of Islam, Hinduism, Buddhism and Judaism. Another failing of many religions has been their inability to tap into a point of resonance or relevance in the lives of ordinary people.

People turning away from religion is not necessarily a bad thing so long as they retain ownership of their spirituality. But sadly this is generally not the case. Many of us spend our lives tumbling in a spiritual vacuum that offers us no purpose or solace. Why is this? And why can't we have spiritual fulfilment without a formal religion? The answer is that this needn't be the case – we can have this sense of spiritual fulfilment without the baggage of religion. The concept of balance that we have been looking at throughout this book culminates in spiritual balance. While the Chinese used the concept of yin and yang to explain balance, their ultimate goal was to show that the entire universe is governed by this principle and at its core is balanced spirituality. The Celts, the Egyptians, the Babylonians, the Mayans, the Native American Indians and all the other great civilisations had spirituality at the centre of their lives. So why is it so difficult to accept that we can be spiritual without following a religion?

I think the answer to this question lies in a very important word – 'ownership'. In the western world and the Middle East, three major monotheistic (one God) religions exist:

Christianity, Islam and Judaism. They share more similarities than differences. They all originated in the Middle East; they all believe in one God; they are all male-dominated; they all share similar beliefs on how fellow man should be treated; and they all believe in a Messiah. However, the concept of ownership is another common denominator between all of these religions. They all claim ownership of their followers' spirituality. Just think about this for a moment. All of these monotheistic religions are basically saying that if you want spirituality then you can get it from them, and them alone, and only on their terms. This makes them no different from the Soviet Union's Communist Party, always insisting they know what's best for you.

By insisting for thousands of years that they alone had a claim over spirituality, the major religions sowed the seeds for the situation we find ourselves in today, where many people have denounced spirituality altogether. This is what lies at the heart of much of the pain, emptiness and disconnection consuming people. Not only do many people not know that they have a right to be spiritual in their own way, independent of religion, but they are not even aware that they have a spirit. It is no wonder then that money has become the new god, with people trying in vain to buy their way out of the spiritual vacuum. But the higher sense of purpose and enlightenment that spirituality promises is not for sale. In fact, recent American research shows that the more money you have the lower your levels of happiness are. The study, which focused on 12,000 people ranging from their freshman year of college to their late thirties, found that those who measured their success in financial terms were generally unhappy. 'If you're not making money, it's much better to be convinced it's not important,' says Norbert Schwarz, a professor of psychology in the University of Michigan who co-authored the study.[49]

The Church's baggage and the lure of a more hedonistic lifestyle are not the only reasons why people are abandoning religion. I believe that one of the strongest push factors is the fact that religion is not holistic in practice. If we can agree that people are made up of four distinct components – mind, body, soul and emotion – when this is overlaid with the Church's doctrine we find that only the needs of the mind are satisfied. The Church is an intellectual entity. While it tells us that we must think of God, it neglects to tell us that we can also experience God in a much wider dimension, through nature and through our bodies, our spirits and our emotions. However, it is important to note that while the Church's focus seems to be on the intellectual, I believe that there are many figures in the traditional Catholic Church who are truly aligned with the spirit. We cannot tar everyone with the same brush. But while it is important to recognise the good and pure aspects of a religion, it is equally important to hold on to our vision and drive when it comes to the areas that need improvement. I believe that it is up to the Church's flock to bring about reform and restore balance between yin and yang, as it is not going to come from the patriarchal leaders.

Thankfully, many of the eastern religions have not lost their connection with the spirit, the mind, the body or the emotions. In fact, these four components form the foundation of some of these religions. Dancing, meditation, art, poetry and physical and spiritual acts are part and parcel of Buddhism, Shinto and Hinduism, to mention but a few. These religions seek to embody God in every action, emotion and thought. As we saw in Chapter 6, the western world is yang-based and, since the mind represents yang, it is clear that western religion has also become mind-based.

In the ancient version of Christianity, the Gnostics and the Celtic Church had a strong mystic tradition. Mysticism is the yin; it is the part without rules or boundaries; it is the unknowable; it is enlightenment. The ancient Christian Church had many powerful mystics who possessed healing and metaphysical abilities as well as powers of clairvoyancy. There was St Teresa of Avila in Spain, Meister Ekhart in Germany and many more. The Christian Church boasted thousands of mystics in the past so why don't we hear of any today? Surely this age should have as many as the previous ages? Or is it simply that the mystics still exist but the present-day yang-based Church is threatened by what it does not understand and refuses to acknowledge them? Judaism also has a little-known mystic tradition known as Kabbalah that is shunned by the establishment, yet for thousands of years it has formed an essential part of the faith.

It would seem that down through the ages all of the great monotheistic religions have become theological and intellectual concepts and have lost their connection with the yin and the people. Catholicism, one of the most intellectual of all the religions, is centred around the idea of transubstantiation. This is the belief that during mass the bread and wine, representing the body and blood of Christ, are transubstantiated and become the actual body and blood of Christ. This spiritual transformation is beyond the mind's grasp. It is a mystical event that defies the laws of physics. When a religion concentrates on the intellectual self rather than the spiritual, physical or emotional selves, it is neglecting the majority of a person's being.

THE GOD QUESTION

Of course this argument about religion presupposes that there is a God. And if God exists, is God a he, a she, both, or a state of consciousness? Perhaps one of the most fascinating questions of all is what is God? If we approach this question from the perspective of the intellect or the yang, what can we learn? Professor Stephen Hawking, one of the finest scientific minds of our time, is the author of *A Brief History of Time*. In this acclaimed book, he proposed the Big Bang Theory as the creation point of the universe. Hawking struggles with the idea of God, wavering between belief and disbelief. However, the following extract from the book is very insightful:

> Even if there is only one possible unified theory (the unifying of the theory of gravity and quantum physics), it is just a set of rules and equations. What is it that breathes fire into the equations and makes a universe for them to describe?

Hawking is obviously trying to give a context to what lies behind the formulae and theories. I think that this reflects our big question. I believe many of us are seeking to place our lives in some sort of context. We are searching for the backdrop, the stage, the writer and the director in the play of our life. So is God just a convenient way to explain all that we cannot explain or is there evidence of a greater power? And if this greater power exists, what shape or form does it inhabit?

I was reared a Catholic in the Christian religion. As a child, I read religious books, attended mass and was educated in the ways of the Church. All this time, God was referred to as a man, as the father. Like many children, I probably imagined him to be a very old man, with a long beard, who lived in the clouds. I never actually stopped and asked myself, does God really look like that? Is God male? Does he live in the clouds? We are taught not to ask these questions. This brings us back to the issue of ownership: we'll tell you how it is, how you should practice and what you should believe in. The real-life image of God that most Catholics are familiar with is that of the old man with the silver beard reaching out to Adam on the ceiling of the Sistine Chapel in Rome. He looks a little like Santa Claus or some benevolent uncle or grandfather in this painting. Michelangelo's depiction of God has been adopted by the masses. However, when addressing artists in the Sistine Chapel, Pope John Paul II said, 'We ought not to imagine that the Divine being is like gold or silver or stone, an image graven by human art and thought.' By this he probably meant that God is beyond our ability to represent. If this is the case, who is to say that God is not a woman? The pope's comment shows us both where we have been going wrong and how deeply ingrained the yang element has become. Recently, I went to mass in my local Catholic church and was amazed by what I heard. Having gone to mass somewhat irregularly most of my life, I had never really analysed the content of the sermon. I now counted 104 references to God using the masculine terms of 'Father', 'He', 'His' and 'Lord'. No female pronouns were used to refer to God. The only token feminine mention in the ceremony was the word Mother which was used three times when talking about Mary, the mother of Jesus. Our society has been subliminally programmed to believe that the male is all-powerful. It is no wonder we find this huge imbalance in the world around us. The yin is denied a meaningful or active representation in monotheistic religions and this has created a spiritually unbalanced society.

This was not always the case. Parts of the Jewish tradition, out of which Christianity was born, contained a Mother God as well as a Father God. Shekinah was the feminine representation of the glory of God. This idea of there being a feminine aspect to God even existed at a time when men thanked God, as part of their morning prayers, that they had not been born a woman. For the Greeks, this feminine energy was represented by Sophia, in all her wisdom and knowledge; the Romans had Juno, the wife of Zeus; the Buddhists had, and still have, Kwan Yin, the feminine deity of Buddha; the Hindus have Lakshmi, the feminine balance of Vishnu, again a present-day deity; the Native American Indians have Mother earth; the Norse and Germans had Freyja; the Egyptians had Isis; and the Celts had the Goddess Bridget, who later became St Bridget in early Celtic Christianity. All of these religions, which were almost entirely disconnected from one another by land and sea, arrived at the same conclusion: that God was both male and female deities balancing one another. We must ask ourselves why all of these people believed that their religion should consist of the two energies, yin and yang. I am not suggesting that the ancient world was perfect. It most certainly wasn't and we should be thankful that many of the practices belonging to those periods have died out. However, we would do well to learn certain lessons from our ancestors and to reclaim our spiritual heritage. The feminine aspect of our spirituality, the yin, has been lost, leaving us with only half the picture and this is why millions of people are turning away from religion.

Most theologians and historians agree that men have largely dominated society during the last two millennia. This explains the ignoring of the feminine energies in religion and ultimately our spirituality. Quite simply, it has always been in the interest of those in power to limit entry to the 'establishment' and allow it to remain a male-controlled domain. Why share power if you can avoid it? There is plenty of documented evidence to show that the Bible, which forms the basis of the Christian faith, has been edited and rewritten to suit the male agenda. The early Church elders, all men, voted on what should be called gospels and what should be considered to be the words of Jesus. As a male-only council it would make sense that they would downgrade the role of the feminine. Also remember that these early Church members were in many cases people of the Roman Empire and as such would have had a very Roman view of the role of women, which is to say that they should not hold positions of power or influence. The Bible as we know it comes from what is often referred to as the 'faith of our fathers'. Margaret Starbird in her book on Mary Magdalene says, 'there is evidence that portions of the four gospels were deleted, added and even censored over the centuries.'[50] The early fathers of the Church believed that equality was heresy and the thought that women could hold clerical positions was considered out of the question. Yet for thousands of years, most of the preceding religions, including some Roman sects, had high priestesses and most certainly recognised the role of the goddess and therefore the feminine influence.

Perhaps the most poignant story that demonstrates the suppression of the feminine in the western world is that of Mary Magdalene. We were introduced to her in the previous chapter as the bride of Christ who was forced into exile and is reputed to have fled through Egypt to the southern shores of France. Hers is the story of the dominance of yang. Her energy is the archetype of the Sophia or goddess, it is the long-lost piece we need to complete ourselves spiritually, which is to say the yin or the sacred feminine energy. Many of the ancient religions I have already mentioned contained the idea of *hieros gamos*, or the sacred marriage; from the husband and wife Osiris and Isis in Egyptian mythology to Mother earth and Father Sky in Native American Indian mythology. The Nag Hammadi Gospels found in the desert suggest how important Mary was to Jesus and also hint that they shared an intimate relationship. When Mary is mentioned in the canonical gospels of the Catholic Church she is, bar once, listed first in the list of Marys and other women in the Bible. She is the first to be mentioned when Jesus is on the cross and it is to her that

Jesus first appears after the resurrection. Mary's pre-eminence in the text is proof of her importance in Jesus' life. It is also pertinent that even though the early Church fathers branded Mary a prostitute, they still did not remove her entirely from the Bible. More than 2,000 years after the death of Jesus and Mary Magdalene, the truth is finally emerging. Through academic research and popular culture, Mary is gaining acceptance as the bride of Christ and as the yin balance in spirituality. Martin Luther believed that Jesus and Mary Magdalene were married, as did Mormon patriarch Brigham Young. Even the Catholic Church themselves in 1969 after centuries of branding Mary Magdalene a prostitute, rolled back from that position saying that in fact she had been mixed up with another Mary. Mary Magdalene inspires new hope that the long-lost feminine balance is finally returning.

Another source of hope for the rejuvenation of the feminine energy comes in the form of Barack Obama's election as president of America. He possesses many strong yin qualities that go some way towards balancing America's yang culture. The need for balance between our leaders and the land they govern has been a consideration since the dawn of time. The Arthurian legends make repeated references to the quest for the 'holy grail'; the holy grail being a chalice used by Jesus at the Last Supper. In the old world, the chalice represented the feminine; it was the womb; the holder of things; yin; the cup of life that would nourish and restore. The king represented the blade – the warring masculine or yang energy. The story goes that God appeared to King Arthur in a vision and told him to find the grail. This grail, God said, would heal the land of England which at the time was beset by crop failures, riots, strife and unhappiness. We can view this legend as an analogy for the absence of yin from leadership. The king represents men and the grail represents the long-lost feminine energy.

I believe that we are witnessing a spiritual revolution. As Margaret Starbird says in her book *Mary Magdalene: Bride in Exile*, 'As we leave the old paradigm of masculine dominance and patriarchal hegemony, passing over into the age to come, we must obey the request of Jesus to follow the man carrying the pitcher of water (Mark 14:13). He is the water carrier Aquarius – the zodiac sign of the next 2,000-year journey that the human family has embarked on.'[51] In astrology as well as the Bible the return of the water carrier or sign represents the return of the feminine or yin which will bring balance to the yang.

REINCARNATION

Reincarnation is the belief that a soul or spirit is reborn into another body after death. The Collins *New English Dictionary* defines 'reincarnation' as the belief that after death the soul is reborn in a new body. It is core to Hinduism and Buddhism and many ancient belief systems. Reincarnation is part of our soul's journey, which over many lifetimes, discovers and reunites with God, source or intelligence. When a soul learns its lessons from each lifetime, such as forgiveness, love, and hope, it is said to be enlightened. The Buddha is held to be the first person to have been enlightened and so stopped reincarnating as his lessons were learned. The subject of reincarnation allows us to ask certain questions of ourselves:

What of our own spiritual journey?

How do we view ourselves in terms of the spirit?

If you believe that you have a spirit or a soul where do you believe it goes when you die?

Where did it come from in the first place?

Do all souls that leave the earth plane evaporate?

Do they go to heaven?

Do they go to hell?

Do they come back?

Physics teaches us that we can neither create energy nor destroy it; it merely changes form. For example, the energy latent in food is released when a farmer eats it, the farmer then has the energy to plough the land, which turns the soil, which activates the soil, and so on. So all the energy that ever was and ever will be is already here on this planet. If we apply this scientific principle to the matter of life and death it raises interesting questions: if a living person contains energy, what happens to this person's energy when they die? If the energy cannot be destroyed, it must go somewhere.

Reincarnation goes against the doctrine of established western religions. However, if there is one thing that this investigation into yin and yang has hopefully taught us, it is that we should always maintain an open and inquisitive mind. One of the most striking things about reincarnation is that for 1.8 billion people this concept is central to their religions, namely the eastern religions of Hinduism, Sikhism, Buddhism and Taoism. Many of these ancient religions share similarities with indigenous tribes who also believed in reincarnation. Again, it is an amazing coincidence that the Native American Indians, the Celts, the Aborigines, the Egyptians, the Aztecs and the tribes of the Far East all shared this belief. Despite being separated geographically they still arrived at the same conclusion. It is only the modern western world that has ruled out the possibility of reincarnation. Perhaps it is the strong grip that the beliefs of Christianity have on its followers that has prevented most of us from even considering the possibility. There was a time when western religions were more open to the concept of reincarnation. The Gnostics and Cathars, who we met earlier, certainly believed in reincarnation, as did many of the Greek scholars such as Plato.

So is there any evidence to support the belief in reincarnation? Dr Stevenson of the University of Virginia, devoted forty years of his life to the scientific documentation of this phenomenon. He recorded over 3,000 cases of young children who claim to have had a previous life. These children, who were not hypnotised or under any duress, spoke openly about the life they had led before they died. They recalled people, places and events from all over the world in detail that should have been beyond their knowledge much less their comprehension at such young ages. Some critics claim suggested memory. But Stevenson was able to ascertain that this was the first time that most of these children had spoken in detail about their memories. He was later able to verify the accuracy of the details of their past lives. One of Dr Stevenson's peers, Dr Harold Lief, wrote of him in the *Journal of Nervous and Mental Disease*, 'Either Dr Stevenson is making a colossal mistake, or he will be known as the Galileo of the twentieth century'

The type of cases encountered by Dr Stevenson (1918–2007) would all have been similar to the following:

The Case of Iranga. The child was born in a village of Sri Lanka near but not on the west coast, in 1981. When she was about three years old she spoke about a previous life at a place called Elpitiya. Among other details, Iranga mentioned that her father sold bananas, there had been two wells at her house, one well had been destroyed by rain, her mother came from a place called Matugama, she was a middle sister of her family, and the house where the family lived had red walls and a kitchen with a thatched roof. Her statements led to the identification of a family in Elpitiya, one of whose middle daughters had died, probably of a brain tumor, in 1950. Among forty-three statements that Iranga made about the previous life, thirty-eight were correct for this family, the other five were wrong, unverifiable, or doubtful. Iranga's village was fifteen kilometers from Elpitiya. Each family had visited the other's community, but they had had no acquaintance with each other (or knowledge of each other) before the case developed.[52]

Many people may also have heard of Dr Brian Weiss through his book *Many lives, Many masters* and his featured TV appearance on *The Oprah Winfrey Show* on 13 May 2008. A graduate of Columbia University and Yale Medical School, Brian L. Weiss, MD, is Chairman Emeritus of Psychiatry at the Mount Sinai Medical Center in Miami. As a traditional psychotherapist, 'Dr Weiss was astonished and sceptical when one of his patients began recalling past-life traumas that seemed to hold the key to her recurring nightmares and anxiety attacks. His scepticism was eroded, however, when she began to channel messages from "the space between lives", which contained remarkable revelations about Dr Weiss' family and his dead son. Using past-life therapy, he was able to cure the patient and embark on a new, more meaningful phase of his own career.'[53] Since then he has worked with thousands helping them to release phobias and fears that are associated with violent death in a previous life. During the show with Oprah he also hypnotised and carried out a past life regression with Dr Mehmat Oz the show's resident doctor who is Vice Chair and Professor of Surgery at Columbia University. Dr Oz admitted that while being sceptical at the beginning, he did indeed have a past life memory and could connect it to aspects of his life today.

Whether or not you believe in reincarnation is not important. If you simply accept that it is a possibility this will have massive implications for how you live your life. Reincarnation inhabits the world of yin. It is an endless cycle of birth, death and rebirth based on the premise that we are all spirits having human experiences rather than human beings having spiritual experiences. If you were to follow this concept you would believe that your behaviour and all your actions and inactions in this life have an impact on the next. Or that your behaviour in your last life is responsible for the good or bad luck you experience in this one. In other words, you are caught in a circle of karma. This idea of karma is bound up in the Hindu religion in the notion of *dharma*. *Dharma* is your life purpose; it concerns the lessons of this lifetime that you are here to learn. In the western world, the area of coaching and personal development call this 'living your truth' or finding your purpose. The language may differ but the behaviour and state of being is the same. The aim is to reach a state of enlightenment, where the purpose of your existence is to serve others and to find personal fulfilment.

If we were to embrace our yin sides and open ourselves up to the possibility that our actions may have everlasting consequences, what would we do differently? The Buddhists answer this beautifully in the following concept. Why kill your enemy when he will just return in another life form, his evilness fully intact. Instead, if you show your enemy compassion and open his heart then you will bring a halt to the cycle of violence or *samsara*. *Samsara* is an endless wheel recycling our mistakes from previous lifetimes and each time we come back we face a bigger lesson until we learn the error of our ways. Imagine how this philosophy would transform our lives if we were to embrace it. Imagine how it would transform society. We would see a global shift from the current hunt for success to a concentration on healing humanity.

It is my belief and hope that we can all find our balance. By taking ownership of our spirituality we will find contentment and fulfilment in our lives. We are on the cusp of a new age. What sort of legacy will we pass on to our descendants 1,000 years from now? Will they say we abandoned the feminine or that we embraced it? The answer to this question lies in our hands.

EXERCISE

The following exercise will help you to initiate a dialogue with your soul.

In a quiet, meditative state answer the questions listed below. Ask yourself the same question seven times, each time allowing the answer to surface naturally in your consciousness. These questions are deep, powerful and profound and are aimed at each of your seven chakras. You may wish to concentrate on one chakra at a time. Keep a notepad close by and record the information you receive. You could also carry out this exercise with a partner, recording your thoughts and observations as you go along. Regular repetition of this exercise will allow you to commune with your spirit and to access the depths of your soul. Enjoy it and allow yourself to ease into a meditative state.

The first time you ask yourself each question, imagine that you are bathed in red light and focus your awareness on your groin and hip area – your root chakra:

Question 1: Who am I?

Question 2: Why am I here?

Question 3: What is my purpose?

Question 4: What does my feminine yin energy want?

Question 5: What does my masculine yang energy want?

The second time you ask yourself each question, imagine you are bathed in orange light and focus your awareness on your belly/lower back area – your sacral chakra.

Repeat questions 1–5.

The third time you ask yourself each question, imagine you are bathed in yellow light and focus your awareness on your solar plexus or mid back – your solar chakra.

Repeat questions 1–5.

The fourth time you ask yourself each question, imagine you are bathed in green light and focus your awareness on the centre of your chest and upper back – your heart chakra.

Repeat questions 1–5.

The fifth time you ask yourself each question, imagine you are bathed in blue light and focus your awareness on your neck – your throat chakra.

Repeat questions 1–5.

The sixth time you ask yourself each question, imagine you are bathed in purple light and focus your awareness on your brow – your brow chakra.

Repeat questions 1–5.

The seventh time you ask yourself each question, imagine you are bathed in violet light and focus your awareness on the crown of your head – your crown chakra.

Repeat questions 1–5.

Chapter 10

The Momentum for Change

Awakening the Collective Consciousness

Humanity is on the cusp of a revolution but whether this revolution comes in the form of a renaissance or Armageddon is largely dependent on us. The changes that are afoot are the direct result of the imbalance that currently exists in the world. We have seen how this imbalance manifests in our health, our relationships, our businesses, the environment and of course our spirituality. Fundamentally, the suppression of the yin lies at the root of the problem. This suppression has been happening both intentionally and unintentionally for so long now that the domination of the yang has become normal, par for the course. It is all we have ever known.

To grasp the enormity of the change that is coming we must think back to the days of Galileo and his assertion that the world was round. We are talking about the awakening of the collective consciousness of humanity – an awakening that has already begun. One day people will look back on this period in history as the spiritual revolution. It will be comparable to the Stone Age, the Iron Age, the Renaissance, the Industrial Revolution and more recently the technological revolution. It is the next step in our evolution as a species. Our current yang way of thinking is nearing the full swing of the pendulum. We must now swing in the opposite direction, towards the feminine way of life.

Depending on your perspective, you will see a world that is evolving and in a state of flux, or you will see a world that is about to fall apart. It is the seer who defines reality. If enough people believe that we are in the grip of a crisis then that is exactly where we will find ourselves. It will become a self-fulfilling prophecy. The social, economic and political systems in operation in the world depend almost entirely on the sentiment of the people. If we all believe that we are in a recession, then the market will collapse. Our modern Keynesian economies work on the basis of supply and demand or scarcity. The scarcer the commodity, the higher the asking price. But what would happen if people stopped believing in the banks or in the value of money? All it would take is for the majority of us to no longer place our trust in the powers that be and these institutions would quickly fall. We are currently witnessing this phenomenon in the banking sector. People are losing faith in the banks and as a result the value of the banks' shares are plummeting worldwide. Even government intervention cannot stop this downward spiral. I believe that deregulation and greed are responsible for the lack of balance in this sector. We, the customers, are playing the role of nature and redressing this imbalance by no longer investing in these institutions. This reduces their credibility in the market and, in the long run, will hopefully lead to a more tightly controlled banking sector.

Our opportunity now, since the status quo has been broken, is to reinvent the banking and economics model. We have a chance to create a world driven by capitalism with a conscience, to build a business and banking model that is balanced and encourages entrepreneurship and commerce but not greed and ego, a model that places the good of society on the same level as profit. In this way we can create a realistic and empathetic model. Sweden has already moved towards this, with strong enterprise but also high tax which supports excellent community programmes and betterment for all. Just in case you think that the Swedes might be unhappy about this, they rank eighth out of ninety-five nations in the World Database of Happiness from Erasmus University, Rotterdam, Holland.

Many of the major cornerstones of the modern western world are crumbling. Political scandals abound and stories of underhandedness and greed dominate our news headlines. Our religious institutions have also offered up their share of headlines in recent years. The Catholic Church, for example, has gone through a major catharsis that will hopefully, in time, yield a stronger, better Church. While some religions have been hijacked by radicals and are being dragged down a dark path, others are restoring balance by cleaning out the misguided yang elements.

Then there are the financial institutions. As previously mentioned, the present-day banking system is becoming obsolete. The idea of a bank charging you to hold your money, which they then loan out at a profit to themselves, but not to the customer, angers many. So much so that new alternative banks such as the online ones are taking over. Online banks, because they have very low overheads, are offering an alternative to main-stream banking with lower bank charges and higher rates for savings. Larger merchant banks, once the darlings of Wall Street, are suffering greatly in the wake of the sub-prime mortgage crisis. The giant pyramid scheme that is inter-bank lending has essentially come a cropper. The banking system has realised that it has loaned far more money than it owns hence the frenzied selling of bank stocks.

The banks owe this mess to their yang-driven greed. The projects they loaned money to were largely yang-based commercial operations and rarely, if ever, humanitarian organisations that served a greater good. The universal law of balance has struck. The banks that survive this storm will be the ones that embrace the yin; in other words, those who actually start looking after their customers and who use their resources to create a better and more equitable society.

A fascinating and bold move by Saddam Hussein in 2000, three years before the Iraq War, when the US invaded and occupied Iraq, helps to put the current global finance issue into perspective. Saddam Hussein was preparing to sell oil by the barrel in euros.[54] This may not seem like much to most. However, if you are the American government there could not be a worse scenario, as your currency is put under pressure and its circulation reduced, possibly destabilising your exchequer. Saddam succeeded in selling oil in euros when the UN approved this move. As we know the US invaded Iraq in 2003, overthrowing Saddam and converting sales of all Iraqi oil back into dollars. This story illustrates the link between business and war, a yang-based approach that is hell-bent on economic empire building and expansion.

When people talk about the end of the world as we know it, I believe they are talking about a shift so huge that it will redefine civilisation. That which is broken will be fixed and that which is out of balance will find equilibrium. The momentum for change has never been greater. The world is riddled with cracks. Our climate is changing with potentially catastrophic consequences, our religious institutions have fallen from grace and the people we once looked to for leadership are being exposed as corrupt and self-motivated. The masses who once so diligently toed the line are now looking for change. And I believe this change is upon us. We have seen the West become the East and the East become the West. The huge communist states of the USSR and China are all but gone, replaced by thriving capitalist societies. Russia, the 'old enemy' as it was once known, is now a major trading partner. Fifty years ago nobody could ever have imagined such changes.

So what will the world be like in another fifty years time? What kind of society will we bequeath to our children? The one certainty is that it will be very different to the one we inhabit today. Once we accept that change is inevitable then our capacity to affect the future increases dramatically. We must accept responsibility for the current state of the nation if we are to rectify our errors and create a new future.

It is human nature to grow and develop. Try and hold your breath for a few minutes and you will quickly see that we are creatures of motion. If our hearts stop and our blood ceases to flow, we will die. Another analogy for this lies in the sprightly seventy-year-old who goes walking every day, plays chess, meets up with friends and goes ballroom dancing. Now what happens if this person has a bad fall and their mobility is compromised? Often they can no longer look after themselves and may require outside assistance, care or even a move to a nursing home or sheltered accommodation. We will see that when movement is lost, the mental faculties, the emotional state and the spiritual state often deteriorate rapidly. It is not uncommon that after such a misfortune this person will soon be of another world. Many of us can relate this example to elderly relatives.

Since the dawn of man, movement has been central to our day-to-day lives. As cave dwellers, we were constantly chasing after the migrating herds and seeking new hunting grounds. To survive we needed to find these new lands and space, as many of the places we lived could only ever support a limited number of people. This caused us to be travellers. It also assisted our evolution as we encountered new mates and kept the gene pool expanding. To move was to survive. Since the invention of the wheel, we have strived to create bigger, better and faster means of transportation. So, as you can see, movement is not so much a choice for us as a prerequisite. It is this same movement and drive that we must use to create change. Interestingly, these are yang or male impetuses. While the feminine energy provides us with the motivation for change, in the form of a desire to correct injustice and create balance, it is the masculine energy that creates the action.

The motivation for change is very personal and will be dictated by our emotions. These emotions form a scale, with love and fear at its two extremities. If we feel we have to change because we are jealous of someone or worried about our future or angry about the state of the world, then any action we take comes from a place of fear. This is very dangerous, as fear feeds the ego and the ego is the master of destruction. No war has ever been started on the basis of love. Greed, envy, insecurity and fear of losing power are generally to blame. So if we go into this era of uncertainty driven by fear, then war and strife will result.

However, we have a choice in the matter. We can choose the positive side of the scale and approach the future from a place of forgiveness, compassion, confidence, optimism, peace and ultimately love. Love unites people and builds the foundations for a wonderful shared future. One of the most moving examples of the power of love was when Colin Parry, the father of schoolboy Tim Parry who was killed by an IRA bomb on 20 March 1993 in Warrington, UK, met with Gerry Adams, the leader of the political arm of the IRA on 1 November 2007. The two men shook hands and in that moment Colin Parry initiated a dialogue with a party whose military arm had perpetrated the attack. Later, when he was asked why he did it, Colin replied that it is easier to talk than to fight. It was Colin's love for his son Tim that enabled him to forgive the men he believed were behind the murder.[55] Colin later set up the Tim Parry Johnathan Ball Foundation for Peace to help those who had suffered similar losses to find resolution and forgiveness. All of these actions stemmed from love. What good would revenge have done Colin? It might have temporarily satisfied his ego, but down the line this same ego would have consumed him with rage and anger. The road of revenge runs along the dark side of the yang while the road of love runs through yin. The latter may not always be the easiest option, but the final destination is infinitely more preferable.

So what is your motivation to change yourself and the world around you? Will you wait until the pain and frustration is so great that it overcomes your apathy? Or will you look to those you love and initiate change in the name of love and for the benefit of the world?

When you start out upon this road to change, insecurity and doubt can easily distract you. We live in a society driven by peer pressure so you may feel that if others are not contributing then how will we ever achieve anything? But if everyone thought this way nothing would ever get done. As the old Chinese proverb says, 'The journey of a thousand miles starts with one step.' The fear that so often cripples us works along the same lines as the divide-and-conquer strategy: if you feel you are going to be the only one, you are less likely to venture outside of the protection of the group. This is where the balance of yin and yang is crucial. The yin offers you an inner sanctuary – a place to retreat to and build your motivation. The power and energy of the yang is necessary to generate the action that will lead to change. What may seem like a small and insignificant step now can have a positive knock-on effect and lead to incredible change in the future. Think of a telescope. If you adjust the angle by just one degree you can find yourself looking at an entirely different galaxy. Small steps can lead to big results. The more people who take these steps, the greater the momentum will be, until eventually it is a tidal wave, unstoppable in its path towards creating positive change.

A tipping point is fast approaching and the imbalance of our world, like a swinging pendulum, will reach its zenith. When this happens there can be only one outcome. The pendulum will change direction as the laws of physics and nature restore balance. We will see this change manifest in attitudes towards the environment, in the food and resource wars, in the collapse of the old guard and the institutions of finance and faith. Those who have become the most unbalanced, be they people or organisations, will be the first to see these changes.

It may seem like a coincidence that this revolution is taking place at a time when there is so much upheaval in the world. But is it a coincidence? If we look at what the ancients had to say we uncover some intriguing predictions. These predictions come from a wide and varied set of cultures and belief systems, but they share a remarkable number of similarities. Some of them may seem fanciful and vague and, in isolation, perhaps they are. However, if we bear in mind that they originated in times and geographical areas completely separated from one another, then we begin to uncover something incredible. The soothsayers, philosophers, visionaries and mystics of the past had a great deal to say about our future.

Firstly, we have the Mayans, an ancient and sophisticated race who were highly skilled in architecture, agriculture, mathematics, astronomy and astrology. They based their calendar on their astral knowledge and it is now recognised as one of the most accurate calendar systems ever produced. It needed to be corrected by only one day in 380,000 years. The calendar ends on 21 December 2012. On this winter solstice the sun will cross through the centre of the Milky Way. The significance of this to the Mayans will never perhaps be known, but many theorists believe that in their eyes it signified an end of days. If you are apocalyptic in your views then this is bad news. Personally, and through my research for this book, I believe it marks the starting point of new phase of our evolution that will see us become more spiritual, more balanced and happier. Like any birth there may be labour pains, but it will be worth it as we move from an outdated yang-only approach to a balanced view of yin and yang in harmony.

In western astrology we are on the cusp of the Age of Pisces, which is coming to an end, and the Age of Aquarius which is just beginning. Each age lasts 2,000 years. We won't actually enter the Age of Aquarius until 2400. However, as the renowned astrologer Andrew Smith explains, 'A cusp is like travelling between countries or borders. As you drive from Germany to France you will notice French-sounding place names becoming more common, food becomes more

French and so on, yet you are still in Germany.'[56] So even though we can feel the energy of the Age of Aquarius, we are still in the Age of Pisces. A picture of a water carrier represents the sign of Aquarius so, drawing on what we know about global warming, could we be entering an age plagued by rising sea levels. In the New Testament of the Bible, Jesus speaks about the Age of Aquarius: 'A man will meet you carrying an earthen pitcher of water; follow him into the house where he goes in' (Luke 22:10; Mark 14:13). Many scholars believe this is the announcement of the Age of Aquarius. Christ himself was seen as heralding the Age of Pisces. He was often referred to as the 'fisher of men' or the 'fisher king'. The astrological symbol for Pisces is the fish and, during their time of persecution, Christians used the symbol of the *vesica pesces* (meaning bladder of a fish) to identify themselves to other Christians. This fish symbol features a lot in medieval Christian art.

The Hindus, on the other hand, follow a Vedic astrology system and they believe that we are at the start of the Satya Yuga – the age of truth. The following is a quote from the Vedas (the Hindu holy books):

Then he will disappear from the face of the earth and she will be without any sovereign and be filled with robbers. There will be incessant rain, for six nights and it will rain and rain and the whole earth will be deluged; no traces of men, houses and trees. After this the Twelve Suns will rise simultaneously and by their rays the whole water will be dried up and the earth will become level.

The Vedas, the Bible and the astrological data all seem to point towards impending change brought on by water. So are we entering the end of our days, as many of these ancient cultures seem to predict? I believe that we are, but not in the sense the doomsday prophets would have us believe. These stories, like many others of that time, are possibly parables and the specific references to water may be purely symbolic.

The element water represents spirituality, so if we take a second look at the Vedic text we could conclude that the rain and flooding signifies the mass spiritual enlightenment of the world. I believe that the Age of Aquarius symbolises the end of ignorance. We can also interpret water as a metaphor for cleansing and new birth. It is used in baptism and in dreams it represents emotion and spirit. In biology, water is our lifeblood. It is the yin element and it is intrinsically linked with spirituality, through holy water, sacred rivers such as the Ganges and the beauty of waterfalls and the sea, that touches our souls. Floods, on the other hand, represent massive and widespread change. Lastly, we have the tides, controlled by the gravitational pull of the moon.

I believe the metaphorical prediction the ancients were trying to communicate is that the old will be washed away and that a new age will enter with all the ease and purity of water. The water carrier is leading us towards the house of enlightenment. The new age will be known as the Golden Age – the age when the ego of man will be transformed into a higher purpose and sense of being; the same ego that once caused so much death and destruction. The overpowering yang will finally be balanced.

Every few million years, different species go through phases of quantum evolution and I believe that we are about to enter this very phase. A phase so exciting and dramatic that it will alter the course of history forever. Just as fish evolved into reptiles and then into birds, we too will learn to fly. This flight will see us break free of the bonds of our minds and the constraints of our egos.

Some people argue that the Age of Aquarius and enlightenment started in the 1960s. From The Beatles and Maharishi Mahesh Yogi to the peace movement, it was a decade of cultural revolution and experiential spirituality. As we know though, we are still 400 years away from this new age. So the 1960s were just a tremor – a precursor to an inevitable larger eruption. The energy of the next wave of spiritual hunger has already begun to manifest. Thanks to the wonders of the internet, uncensored writing and a decrease in religious control, this wave will be much bigger and more accessible to the masses. The main eruption will happen in and around 2012. My theory is that this will be the yin revolution. The number of enlightened and forward-thinking people will reach a tipping point and they will raise the level of collective consciousness, propelling us into the next stage of our evolution. Those who are already paying attention to their yin side will thrive. But those who shun the spiritual yearnings of their soul in favour of material gain will find themselves adrift in the new world order. Their material lifestyles will evaporate. I don't believe that they will actually lose their possessions (although they will certainly decrease in value) but rather that they will be cut off from the world's true wealth, its emotional and spiritual gifts and rewards, because they are incapable of opening their eyes to them.

The impetus for change is reaching a crescendo. Never before have so many omens, prophecies and predictions collectively pointed towards change. For those who embrace this change, nirvana awaits. All of the great prophets, from Jesus to Buddha to Mohammed, agreed that heaven is inside of you and is yours to access. My Granddad, who was also a healer, spoke of this path as 'kingdom living, a foretaste of heaven itself'.[57]

The realisation that huge change is afoot is dawning on countless people every day. Through books, the internet, courses, TV and debates, the truth is resurfacing. I see this every day in my work as a coach. People are beginning to see the 'rat race' for what it is and are realising that there must be some other reason why they were put on this planet. It has become a question of life purpose. We are becoming a race of seekers. The yang has been ascending for so long now that we have almost forgotten about the yin. But it runs deep. It is ingrained in our DNA; it is part of the soul or spirit that breathes life into our veins. The yin is like a stream of water trying to find its way to the surface – it will try every crack and crevice until it eventually finds a way through.

For a long time now, people have been experiencing a gnawing feeling that something is not right. Those who are tuned in will turn to religion, personal development, meditation or other sources of information that try to help them understand the subconscious. The lucky amongst them will find their true voice and purpose. When this happens, it is a moment so precious and beautiful that it will never be forgotten. It is the realisation of the self as a spirit.

Those who ignore the gnawing feeling and surrender to the ego and the yang will be plagued by cravings and addictions – cravings for material goods, sex, drugs, alcohol, fame, money and power. All of these things are illusions of the self. They are transient. They don't grant you access to the spirit or the soul, but instead corrupt the opportunity every individual has to get to know God and their higher spirit. This fork in the road, where yin and yang branch off, is dividing the world. A two-tier system is developing, with those who are aware and care on one level and those who don't on the other. In some ways it can be seen as a battle between good and evil; the good being represented by enlightenment and truth, and the bad by ignorance and a tyrannical need to control fellow man.

Once the yin energy starts to rise in you, your journey has begun. It may begin with the question, 'Why am I here?' While this seems like a simple question, it is in fact incredibly profound and complex. However, if you succeed in answering it you will discover your true purpose. Yin and yang are about the divine dance, the fluid synchronicity of the male and female energies. Radha and Krishna represent the loving unity of the masculine and feminine energy in the Vedic principles of manifestation. This energy can manifest not only as emotion but also as a physical sensation.

When I first began to think about my work and what I was hearing and experiencing in the world around me, it became crystal clear to me that the masculine yang was overpowering the female yin and causing an imbalance. After investigating further and immersing myself in the world of the yin, I decided to write this book. Initially, a part of my ego enjoyed telling people about my project and hearing them express confidence in me. Without realising it, I was using the yin to gain yang recognition. Moreover, I was dedicating a lot of time to thinking about writing this book but I wasn't actually doing any writing. It was at this point that my subconscious yin began sending me some pretty clear messages.

I sail at international level and play golf on a regular basis, both of which are yang activities. During the period when I should have been writing this book, I suffered injuries to the left side of my body while engaged in these sports. I injured my left shoulder during a sailing manoeuvre on a windy day and while playing golf I slipped and injured my left knee. If you cast your mind back to the section on health you will remember that the left side of the body represents the yin. Around this same time, I was involved in sales development for my business and was experiencing occasional pain in my upper left back. Now sales is about as yang-driven as you can get. I believe that it was no coincidence that all of these injuries befell me during classic yang activities. I should mention that prior to this I have been almost injury free my whole life. To be struck by all these aches and pains in the space of six weeks was a sign. My subconscious yin was using my body to tell me that I had to start this book. As soon as I began writing the symptoms vanished. I had listened to the messenger and understood the message.

What message do you think your yin is sending you? What changes do you have to make to find balance? If you acknowledge the need for change deep inside you, you will receive the key to unlock your life's purpose. The only real question from that point on is 'Who am I?' And this question, if pursued into the depths of your soul, can lead to only one place. Enlightenment.

YOUR HIGHER PURPOSE

To help create this moment of change within you, complete the following exercise. It taps into the energy of the feminine and masculine and will help you to understand your life's purpose.

Preparation:

Find a quiet space where you will not be disturbed for fifteen minutes. Sit on a comfortable chair. Place your hands on your knees and keep your feet flat on the floor. Close your eyes and breathe deeply. Now relax and you are ready to begin.

First, I want you to say out loud, 'Please God, place all my awareness in my heart.' Some of you may struggle with the word god. But we are referring to *your* god. This may be the god of your religion or simply whatever god means to you, be that the greater good, the higher order, divine intelligence or universal love. Go ahead and say this sentence aloud three times. Direct all of your awareness around your spiritual heart which is located in the centre of your chest. Feel yourself connect deeply with your higher heart. Ask yourself out loud, 'What is my purpose?'

Now invite your heart to speak to you and allow any images, thoughts, ideas, sounds, smells, sensations, or anything that will help you understand your higher purpose, to come from your heart. Repeat the question and wait for answers or signs to be revealed.

Chapter 11

The Yin Yang Future

BUILDING THE NEW WORLD ORDER OF PERFECT BALANCE

The future of the human race is uncertain. We could be hit by a meteor similar to that which killed the dinosaurs; we could run out of natural resources; or disease could ravage us. On the other hand a utopian future may await us, full of love, understanding and peace, one that sees unity and consciousness raised to the highest levels and balance between the male and female energies restored. What most of us don't realise is that we have a *choice* in which future awaits us. But either through lethargy, redundant belief systems, apathy or a lack of love many of us don't care about the future. We are too preoccupied with protecting what we have now to worry about the implications for our future and the future of our planet. This way of thinking has been handed down to us from previous ages. But at some stage a generation has to take responsibility and begin working towards a better future. Could our generation be the one to let go of the material obsessions of the ego and ensure a better future for our children and our children's children? I believe that we can and that in some ways we have already started this process.

MEDICINE

So what might the future look like? What would it be like to live there? If we embrace the yin and yang in our nature and try to create balance between the two, we could create an entirely new paradigm for how we live our lives. We would be able to transcend the ego that currently wreaks so much destruction on our society. Physically we need to be healthy and happy. After that we can begin to focus on the external world. It is only after an illness that most of us truly value our health. As they say, 'Your health is your wealth.' If we balance the masculine and feminine qualities of yin and yang in our health we will find ourselves revitalised. When you tune into both energies you can become your own physician. You will become acutely aware of the biorhythms of your body. You will know which foods agree with you, and which don't, and what causes your ailments and how to heal yourself. You will recognise the influence of your emotions, your thought patterns and the spiritual signals that are being transmitted to your physical body. Bioscience pioneers such as Dr Deepak Chopra believe that you can potentially cure any illness through your mind and spirit. By creating a yin and yang balance within yourself, you will be able to live life to its fullest potential.

The ancient Vedic scholars of India believe that every person has the potential to live to be 120 years old and there is also an old Yiddish saying that wishes you 120 years of life. Researchers have found that this should be possible for many in the future. Evolutionary theorist Oliver Curry from the London School of Economics, says that the human race will have reached its physical peak by the year 3000. These humans will be between 6ft and 7ft tall and they will live up to 120 years. I believe that this will happen through a combination of better nutrition, meditation, less stress and better technology and medicine. It will be the reward for embracing both a masculine and feminine approach.[58]

It is interesting to note that the Vedic system classes youth as 0–40, middle age as 40–80 and old age as 80–120. Perhaps you feel a little younger now. This evolution in our approach to medicine will see us make better use of the healing properties of the herbs, plants and minerals that surround us. Currently, over 120 prescription drugs originate in the rainforests but this may be only the tip of the iceberg. If we recognise the true value of the rainforests and work towards saving them rather than destroying them, then they may ultimately save us.

The laying on of hands, which is practised in almost all eastern cultures and many of today's western cultures, will become the norm as we embrace the healing powers of energy and life-force. We will achieve an internal balance through meditation, yoga, the correct diet, an active lifestyle, science-based medicine, healing arts and loving relationships. The new picture of health will serve as a cornerstone for a new way of living. This internal perspective of balance will give rise to an external balance – as within so without. The world around you will become your mirror. The symbiotic balance between humans and nature will reach out and touch every living thing, creating a vibration of harmony as the powerful forces of yin and yang lead us towards a future full of health and vitality.

RELATIONSHIPS

As we approach life from a point of balance we will begin to see relationships in a new light. Rather than blaming our parents, our ancestors or society for our patterns of behaviour, we will instead look upon them with compassion. We will be grateful for the fact that we can identify these patterns that caused the previous generation so much grief and have the potential to do the same to us. We have the ability to stop history repeating itself by writing a new script for ourselves and our families. We will remove the old doubts, prejudices and negative thought patterns that surrounded people, money, health, religion and so on from the family lineage and karma. By recognising our unique blend and balance of yin and yang energy we will gain self-awareness on a truly profound level. We will know our own energy and allow it to express itself in its unique and beautiful way. In this manner, our true selves will emerge and we will project an image of our higher selves, and not just our ego selves, to the rest of the world.

By no longer observing the media's rules and stereotypes about beauty you will be free to be yourself. No more dressing to impress or adorning yourself in a certain way because you think it will attract a mate or make you more popular. This state of being will allow you to enter relationships on a new level; relationships that are forged by the coming together of true identities. Gone will be the charades and masks we once used to interact with other people. Men and women will respect one another as equal parts of the one whole; as partners who come together in the divine union – the same union that governs nature. In other words, you will find your soul mate or your *anam cara* as it is known in the Celtic tradition. With the ego no longer obscuring your vision, the path to true intimacy will be paved. In this enlightened state of being we will see a reduction in the rate of divorce, unhappy relationships and mistrust. By allowing your true self to emerge, that which is divine in you will also emerge. As Jesus said, 'No one lights a lamp and puts it in a place where it will be hidden, or under a bowl. Instead, he puts it on its stand, so that those who come in may see the light' (Luke 11:33). If your light is visible, then so too is your true self. The balance of yin and yang will allow love to blossom and the divine nature to emerge. In this way you will fulfil a part of your destiny and create situations of mutual love and support as you move forward in the world.

Out of this union the next generation is born. They are our legacy and our hope for the future. If we take action now, it is possible that they will not suffer the same imbalances that have marked our period on this earth. I believe that our children are the greatest leverage we have for continued change. In my work as a coach, I find that my clients often baulk at the thought of making alterations in their lives and they struggle to find the right motivation. However, if I tell them that these changes could lead to a better world for their children, they will embrace them, no matter how difficult it may be. This is the yin energy. The energy of nurturing, mothering and supporting. We want what is best for our children. This desire is also underpinned by the biological impetus to protect them as they carry our DNA into the future. By drawing on the yin energy, we can create a better world, but by drawing on the combined strengths of the yin and yang we can bring about profound and lasting change. These changes will manifest in the beliefs, attitudes and values that we imbue in our children. All too often we see negative belief systems passed down from generation to generation.

These can range from racism to materialism to apathy, and so on. However, we shouldn't blame our parents for passing them on to us as most of the time they are unaware that they have done so. Instead, as enlightened and educated people we must take it upon ourselves to revise our belief systems and identify what we do and do not want to retain as part of our family lineage. We can break the cycle of *samsara* (the Sanskrit word for perpetual ignorance). We must arm our children with beliefs that will raise both them and the people around them to a higher plane of existence than we dream of in this lifetime.

EDUCATION

It is important that we have a vision of our children's future so that we can begin to make provisions for it. The word vision derives from the Sanskrit word *vid* meaning knowledge. Our vision of the future must be informed by knowledge. This is why it is so important that we understand both the yin knowledge and the yang knowledge. We need to understand the mystical as well as the scientific, the old as well as the new. Armed with this holistic view, we can create a vision of the future truly worthy of our children. Education will be our starting point.

In the future I believe that the western education system, the Catholic Church and the remaining traces of the Roman Empire will all be replaced. There will be less religious education as spirituality becomes more prominent. We will be rewarded in equal measure for creative subjects and science subjects. And we will work towards enhancing the emotional abilities of the child as much as the intellectual abilities. These changes will benefit each and every child equally by bringing their individual talents to the fore and teaching them how to communicate and work in harmony. Parents and teachers alike will encourage children to fulfil their potential in a system that sees happiness as the key to a balanced child rather than academic or sporting success. As in ancient times, the role of the sage and guru will fall to the elders of the tribe. The archetypes of the wise old man and woman will be revived and they will contribute to this greater cycle of knowledge and insight.

BUSINESS

The business world is the section of our society that harbours the biggest imbalance, with its seemingly insatiable appetite for profit at any cost and a yang energy that is wildly out of control. It is this section that will undergo the greatest changes in the future. While businesses must make a profit, they need to do so in a way that ensures the security and success of the company, but does not lead them to fall into the trap of greed. If we see a person who cannot stop eating they might be accused of gluttony and would be advised to stop eating so much for the benefit of their own health.

As it stands, the business world costs lives. This may sound dramatic but unfortunately it is true. The impact of stress on our health is incredible. It is one of the leading causes of illness in western society. Then there is the cost incurred by families who are spending very little time together because of the demands of hectic work schedules. Lastly, we have the dubious moral character of western business. How many companies are actually working for the benefit of humanity? Only when public opinion changes will these companies be forced to rethink their approach and follow the flow of the new market. They will throw billions into advertising and political lobbying to prevent this from happening, but the fact remains that if you decide not to buy their products or services then they will go out of business. I believe that a new paradigm of business is available. It will revolve around companies that genuinely work for the benefit of humanity. They are the cottage industries of today; the environmentally friendly paper companies; the healthcare innovators who put patients first; the non-profit lending institutions. And yes, non-profit lending institutions really do exist. In various countries all over the world, including the UK, USA and Ireland, credit unions return any profit they make to their members, who are both the account holders and shareholders of the institution. The most remarkable example of such organisations is a micro-credit network in Bangladesh set up by Muhammad Yunus. The Grameen

Bank, as it is known, provides interest-free loans to the poor to enable them to set up small businesses and break free of the poverty trap. The default rate is extremely low and the people who receive these loans benefit remarkably. Yunus was awarded the Nobel Peace Prize for his work. This is a perfect example of a business with a yin and yang balance; the internal drive and desire to help the poor (yin) coupled with the ability to make it happen through clever economics and a sound business model (yang). Compare this set-up with the company Enron and their auditors Arthur Andersen who ultimately collapsed because of corporate greed and a lack of moral principles. In short, there was a complete absence of yin.

I believe that companies with vision and balance similar to the Grameen Bank will define the future of the business world. The ultimate winners will be the companies that embrace a charter to make people's lives better rather than simply profiteering. There will be an end to businesses merely paying lip service to corporate and social responsibilities as a public relations exercise. In the future, success will be measured as much by the contribution a company makes to society as by the figures on their balance sheets. Those who respect the family unit and provide flexible working hours, low-stress environments and fulfilling work will be the ones to succeed, and not just because they are ethically and morally sound, but also because they will attract the best people. It is a win-win situation for the company and the employee. The carbon footprint of a company will also be a marker of success in the future. Imagine how exciting it would be to work for a carbon-neutral employer. It is these companies that will herald the end of the reliance on high carbon energy sources such as oil and gas, replacing them with solar, wind, water and geothermal energy sources.

Already countries are grouping together to ensure that government investments, such as pension funds, do not go to the likes of arms and munitions manufacturers. This has already happened in the case of anti-personnel landmines and cluster munitions. The Cluster Munitions Treaty was adopted in Dublin in May 2008 by 107 states. The treaty's purpose 'prohibits all use, stockpiling, production and transfer of Cluster Munitions. Separate articles in the Convention concern assistance to victims, clearance of contaminated areas and destruction of stockpiles.'[59]

There will no doubt be a backlash. The yang companies will not go down without a fight. But the will of the people and their desire for a better world will prevail. We will all need to work together. While your yin side might be motivated by the argument presented here, you will also need to enlist your yang side if you are going to take action.

Turning your attention to your own employer, ask yourself the following questions. Is your company an ethical investor? Does your company contribute towards making the world a better place? If not, is there a viable alternative? How can you influence your company to be more caring and community-spirited in its approach? In answering these questions, remember that you are part of the solution.

THE COMMUNITY

What kind of societal structure are we heading towards? One possible scenario is that if yin and yang are balanced we will find our world less entrenched by laws. If common decency can prevail then we could be a largely self-policing society. People will seek to live in smaller communities where crime, anti-social behaviour and 'rat race' commuting will be rare. These communities will place a greater emphasis on generating green energy from solar, wind and water sources. Fruit and vegetables will be grown locally, meaning communities will have an abundant supply of food with the added benefit of a low carbon footprint. While many people will still work in large companies, they will choose to reside in these smaller communities. The elders of these groups will impart their knowledge and positive values to the younger generations, helping to improve approaches to education and child rearing. This utopian ideal can be realised by embracing technology rather than shunning it. This is already happening. A good friend of mine owns an old water mill which he is in the process of converting to generate hydroelectric power. He intends to provide free electricity to his immediate neighbours. Why not charge for this electricity you may ask. After he has met his own needs, he will have excess power and he is happier to pass it on to his neighbours than to further line the pockets of the energy companies.

In the future we will see a society where the yin – altruism and community spirit – will assume the same level of importance as the yang – innovation, science and business. The two energies will become symbiotic. The latest technology will go hand in hand with the ways of the olden days. It is interesting to note that Gore & Associates, who produce the high-tech fabric gore-tex and have thousands of employees, always try to keep teams or groups to a maximum of a 150 people. This is because at any time 150 relationships are all we can handle on a daily basis. Gore & Associates will even house the groups separately. If a unit grows to over a 150 people, then a spin-off unit is set up in a new building to help maintain the high levels of teamwork and good working relationships. Also of interest is that no one has a title, all employees are called Associates; this means that there is no hierarchy but there are responsibilities. The end result is that Gore & Associates is extremely successful. This rule of 150 was created by British anthropologist Robin Dunbar who found that twenty-one hunter-gatherer tribes studied from around the world all had average village sizes of 148.4 people per group. It also appears that through military history a unit of 150-200 is the maximum that works effectively together and where each member is known to the others.[60]

The project Tribewanted is an amazing example of what is possible if we combine the old and the new, the yin and the yang. In 2006 the tiny Fijian Island of Vorovoro became the site of a unique social experiment. Ben Keene and Mark Bowness came up with the idea of creating a sustainable eco-community. They assembled an online tribe from which people are regularly selected to go to the real island to integrate with the natives. The members of the online community must declare what skills they can bring to the island and every month new tribe members arrive for a stay that varies from one to twelve weeks. In this time they learn local skills and live as the indigenous tribe do and, in turn, they help with building and education projects. This project has successfully and seamlessly blended an ancient indigenous culture with a modern online community. By embracing both the yin and yang, we can create the cornerstones necessary for stability, knowledge and peace. Happiness and a genuine sense of fulfilment will then blossom on this fertile ground. I believe we will see many more initiatives like Tribewanted in the future.

THE ENVIRONMENT

The possibilities of a greener and more sustainable future for our environment are very exciting. The first and most important leap we need to make is to understand that we are not independent of the world around us. We have cultivated a disconnection from nature that is quite literally unnatural. However, if we invoke the energy of the yin we can tune ourselves back into our environment and, in doing so, help bring an end to global warming. If we look on nature as a cycle that we are part of then we are less likely to pollute and destroy our lands, seas and skies. In the future, more and more people will become concerned about the legacy we are leaving our children and our children's children. We are already seeing indications of this in the move towards alternative energy and sustainable farming.

It is the smaller changes taking place in our society that are most indicative of a tipping point. For example, in 2006 vegetable seeds in the UK outsold plant seeds for the first time ever. This shows that more people are growing their own food and rejecting the genetically enhanced, irradiated fruit and vegetables being sold in supermarkets. Such self-sufficiency is imperative when we see that this year, for the first time since the Second World War, there are massive rice shortages. In March 2008 countries like India, the world's third-largest rice exporter, banned all rice exports (except basmati) to maintain local supplies.[61] Added to this is the fact that most grains and rice are being grown from the same variety of seeds, meaning that one super parasite could potentially wipe out the entire strain of a crop.

Luckily, some people are thinking ahead. Small companies and not-for-profits worldwide are starting seed-saver initiatives to preserve rare and endangered plant, crop and fruit types. In the future, the genetically modified plants may have self-destructed by succumbing to mutated pathogens. Also if there is a lack of variety, with all farmers growing the fast cash-rich crops, then a bacteria or fungus could easily wipe out massive amounts of the same crop. I believe that the people behind these seed-saving initiatives will then hold the keys to recovery. Again it will be the yin that saves the yang. I believe that we will grow far more food as communities and rely less on imported food. Advances in science will mean that we will be able to grow produce that previously needed to be imported using modern materials to protect crops and fruit, and utilising naturally occurring heat sources such as geothermal energy to protect plants from frost. Every day new sensors are helping farmers to use less water in irrigation and can regulate air temperatures in growing tunnels to ensure the best conditions for growth. These systems can be wind and solar powered and will have no carbon impact.

In the more responsible society of the future, the heavy investment in alternative energy sources will provide us with sustainable energy and a zero-carbon footprint. By turning to nature, we will harness the energy of the oceans, the wind and the sun. The future system will differ from the present in that much of the energy will be produced locally rather than in centralised power plants. In fact, the system will be very much the opposite of power plants. Locally produced surplus energy will be fed back into the grid to be circulated to regions that may have weak winds or a lack of sunlight. The future will see us become personally responsible for our energy production and consumption.

SPIRITUALITY

At the heart of all this change lies our spirituality. I believe, without a shadow of a doubt, that the next stage in our evolution is a spiritual awakening. This heightened consciousness will be the bedrock on which a successful future will be built. By embracing spirituality, we can proceed with only the best intentions for our families, ourselves and the world. We have so far caught only rare glimpses of the type of spirituality to which I am referring. These glimpses have taken human form, whether it be Gandhi who fought for freedom from oppression with peace as his only mantra, Mother Teresa who rescued the poor from the gutters of Calcutta, Nelson Mandela who found it in his heart to work with his former oppressors, Rosa Parks whose courage sparked the end of racial segregation in the southern states of America, or anyone else we know who was willing to sacrifice their ego for the good of humanity. These people show us what all of us, without exception, are capable of.

We can all choose to operate from a place of integrity and compassion. By doing so, we will transcend the negativity of the ego and its insatiable appetite for recognition and material success. What few of us realise is that the material things we so desperately seek are empty and meaningless without a spiritual consciousness. This transcension of the ego will open up new levels of knowledge and insight. We will understand each other and the world around us in a way we can scarcely imagine. We will radically change the way we use our minds. At present, science only knows what function is served by 10 per cent of our brains, but I believe that as we continue to evolve the other 90 per cent of our brain's capacity will start to unfold allowing psychic ability and creative insight to be come available to us. We will be able to sense and interpret information and the world on a whole new spectrum.

In my research for this book I came across what is known as the 'Cathar Prophecy'. The Cathars, you may recall, were the Christian sect that prospered in the south of France and were renowned for their links to Mary Magdalene and the masculine and feminine view of Christianity – the yin and yang view. Colin Bloy the founder of Fountain International, a UK-based global healing group, after a visit to Montségur in 1978 wrote the Cathar Prophecy. He claimed that he wrote by intuition and that it is not his own work but rather he simply transcribed it. He believed that a church, in terms of a community of like-minded people rather than a religious group, would be formed in 1986. It is also clear that he believed this was a restoration of the old Cathar way rather than a brand new way. I believe that what Bloy channelled is a very strong reflection of the balance that is promised by the balancing of the yin and yang energies in the world and ourselves. The prophecy describes the future in quite a timeless manner. Every time I read it, I am struck anew by its simple profundity. Here is an extract from the prophecy:

> In accordance with an old prophecy the Church of Love is restored ...
>
> Those who participate, practise the Truth of Love in all their beings.
>
> There is no walk of life or nationality that is a barrier. Those who are, know.
>
> It seeks not to teach but to be and, by being, enrich.
>
> It recognises the collectivity of all humanity and that we are all one with the One.
>
> It recognises that the way we are may be the way of those around us because we are that way.
>
> It recognises the whole planet as a Being, of which we are a part.
>
> It recognises that the time has come for the supreme transmutation, the ultimate alchemical act, the conscious change of the ego into a voluntary return to the whole.

It does not proclaim itself with a loud voice but in the subtle realms of loving.

It salutes all those in the past who have blazoned the path but paid the price.

It admits of no hierarchy or structure, for no one is greater than another.

Its members shall know each other by their deeds and being and their eyes, and by no other outward sign, save the fraternal embrace.

Each one will dedicate his or her life to the silent loving of their neighbour and environment and the planet, whilst carrying out their daily task, however exalted or humble.

It recognises the supremacy of the great idea which may only be accomplished if the human race practises the supremacy of Love ...[62]

This prophecy encapsulates the spiritual wisdom of almost every belief system, tradition and religion. It is a blueprint for a harmonious and peaceful world. It is important to note that the word church does not refer to a religion or place but rather a community united by a common spiritual purpose and understanding.

You have an opportunity to create this future. As quantum physicists tell us, time is not linear, it is only our concept of it that is. This new world – the utopia – is available to you today in your heart. Unite your yin and yang and through the power of love become whole. Become both the question and the answer. Be yin, be yang, be love. Be.

Envisioning Exercise

To envision something is to see it with your minds eye or to imagine a future reality. As we already have seen and heard all energy exists in the world of physics as wavelengths and frequency. We saw that all light and sound can be measured by wavelength and frequency. The resonance of an object is the frequency that it exists at. Even solid objects have a specific frequency. A wine glass may have a resonating frequency of 800Hz which means that if a sound is played towards the glass that has 800 pulses or waves per second, the glass will shatter.[63] If we take this a step further then we can see that all thoughts have a biorhythm and therefore a frequency. These frequencies/thoughts have the power to penetrate through the field of energy that we live in because as we have seen all things are simply made up of resonating frequencies, including ourselves.

When we meditate or visualise we start to put out frequencies or thoughts to the universe that attract to ourselves the things that we desire. We also access the deeper levels of our consciousness and in doing so open up vast mental resources that begin to operate subconsciously to help us achieve our goals. This is why visualisation has become so important in sport. It is also key to helping ourselves to heal by bringing into our awareness that which we wish to have. We all work on the law of attraction which says that what we think we attract to ourselves. Therefore if you think constantly of financial ruin then that is what you attract. This can clearly be seen when you look at boom-bust entrepreneurs who have great skill to make money but always seem to lose it again. Unbeknownst to themselves they will be carrying a pattern of self sabotage or a belief that they are not worthy of success, a classic case of having the right skills but not the right core beliefs. These people create success, but then lose it all because they fear losing it. Fear in their minds is a thought that reoccurs on a regular basis and therefore it is fear-based circumstances or vibrations that they attract into their lives.

What we will do with this exercise is to put into our subconscious and to put out to the universe in the form of thought-based energy and vibration, a vision of what we wish our lives to be about. We have travelled through our yin and yang to gain awareness of ourselves and the world around us. Now it is time to put our yin and yang to work and create the future that we wish.

Envision

Find a quiet space where you will be undisturbed for fifteen minutes. Sit or lie down in a comfortable position. Allow your breathing to settle and find a natural rhythm. When you are ready, begin.

Become aware of a beautiful white light shining above your head. See this light intensify in strength. Feel, see or sense how beautiful this light is.

Slowly see, sense or feel this light move down and touch the crown of your head. As it does you feel a great wave of relaxation, peace and love move down through your body. Feel the light move down behind your eyes, releasing and relaxing any areas of tightness. Feel the light intensify and move down into your face, relaxing your brow, eyebrows, eyes, eyelids, nose, cheeks, ears, jaw, mouth and chin. Feel your tongue soften in your mouth. Feel the light flow down your neck releasing all stress, strain and tension. Feel the walls of your throat soften.

Feel the light spread across your shoulders, while all the time your breathing brings you deeper and deeper into a state of perfect relaxation. As the light moves through your shoulder joints feel them relax. Feel the light move down your upper arms, to your elbows, your forearms, your wrists, your hands, all the way to the ends of your fingers. Your entire arms are now covered in this beautiful light.

Feel, sense or see a wave of light move down your chest and upper back, releasing and relaxing as if goes. Feel the light continue down to your midriff, lower back and into your hips and groin. All the time your breathing is bringing you deeper and deeper into a perfect state of relaxation. Allow the light to gently roll down your legs, across your thighs and hamstrings, to your knees, shins, calves, ankles, across your feet all the way to your toes. You are now completely covered in this beautiful light and you can feel waves of peace and love filling every cell in your body.

You now notice that in front of you is a doorway. You open this door and see that a path has been revealed. You walk along this path that is covered on both sides by tall trees, and sunlight shimmers through the leaves and onto your face as you walk. You notice you are wearing no shoes and can feel warm ground under your feet. After a short walk you come to a clearing and in this clearing stands a stone house with a wooden door. You enter this house and see on entering it, that it is one large and beautiful room with a large bay window at one end. You feel safe and loved and secure in this room.

You walk to the end of the room to the window and through this window you see yourself. You are now watching yourself as a witness and observer. See yourself with completely balanced yin and yang energy. What are you doing? Are you with family, friends or a loved one? Are you engaging in a favourite pastime, sport or hobby? In whatever you are doing see yourself looking happy, peaceful and balanced, enjoying your life. Notice who else is there. What are you wearing? What colours are in this picture? What sounds can you hear?

Now see yourself living a life of balance and success doing whatever it is that you really wish you could do. There are no limits in this place. Do not let age, finance, circumstance or any other barrier stand in your way. What would you be doing? What would the world around you be like?

Now make that image stronger, intensify the colours and sounds, seeing yourself living the life you truly wish for. Now see the picture magnify and increase in size so that you feel you are being drawn into the scene before your eyes. Now allow yourself to merge with this scene. Feel how happy you are here. Feel how your masculine energy feels strong and balanced, feel how your feminine energy feels strong and balanced. Notice the strong sense of happiness and freedom that you feel from this balance of yin and yang. Now increase the intensity of these emotions, really let yourself go and embrace these feelings of love and peace.

Know that these feelings will, can be and are now the feeling state that you choose to live in. With these feelings strongly locked into your memory you now find yourself back in the room. You look out the window at yourself and thank yourself for the vision that you have given yourself of the future. You walk back to the door of the house and out into the clearing. See yourself walking back through the forest and back to the door to your conscious mind. You step through this door and in doing so you take with you all the memories, images, thoughts and feelings that you have experienced. Know that you can return to this place whenever you wish to project into the future that which you wish for, whether that be a relationship, health, wealth, community, environment, career, family, connection with God or simply peace and happiness.

Feel the awareness return to your body. Five, take a deep breath in and notice that you are in your room, chair or bed. Four, gently move your fingers and toes. Three, take another deep breath in, feeling energy rush into your body. Two stretch your hands and feet. One, take a deep breath in and open your eyes feeling fully revitalised.

Well done. You are on the way to creating the future you desire.

Conclusion

Thank you for taking this journey through the ages, yourself and your world using the vehicle of yin and yang. What you may have drawn from the experience is that there is no situation, person, company, environment or place that does not in some way hold the energy of the masculine and feminine. I hope this journey has awakened both your yin and yang energy and in reading this book you have been able to use your yang mental ability and your yin intuitive ability to judge what you have read. Hopefully the work has resonated for you at both these levels.

CONTEXT

These yin and yang energies are all around us and in us and in every breath we take. So often we struggle to make sense of the world and its sometimes volatile and irrational nature. What we are always searching for in our lives, whether it be derived from philosophy, experience, spirituality or other people, is context. When we have a context it grounds our experiences and beliefs and gives us a reference point by which we can understand our world. What *The Yin Yang Complex* has hopefully provided you with is a context for living.

We have looked at the context of our lives and how we each have a balance of masculine and feminine energy. We were able to see the implications and character traits associated with each dynamic. From the yang-driven warrior to the yin-driven mother we have explored the archetypes that reside in our souls. We saw how these energies are manifested in our physical bodies and in the way we move, talk, sleep, eat and live. We saw how ego and empathy can weave together to create a balance that is both caring and action-oriented, and how we each have blueprints for the perfect partner encoded and imprinted into our consciousness. Having found that partner we learned how each energy of yin and yang could manifest in the relationships we form. From the thunderous slow-building energy of the yin to the lightning strike of the masculine energy, we explored how this high tension energy was the spark and dynamic difference that attracts yin to yang and vice-versa.

We have learned how to use the tools and techniques of labyrinths, breathing, meditation, physical stimulus and emotional insights to encourage balance in ourselves on the emotional, physical, spiritual and mental levels. We have seen how the values of the Roman Empire are still alive and well in the boardrooms of today. The impact that businesses are having on the planet and society has been identified, and how the need for balance is urgently required to stabilise them. As I write this there is a small recovery taking place in the world economic markets. In Ireland we are pumping over 50 billion into the Irish banks to keep them stable. The irony is that no major layoffs or redundancies have taken place in this industry, while every other industry from airlines to accountancy firms are shedding jobs rapidly. This goes to show who really runs the country, when the people can be taxed to bail out those who caused the crash in the first place with their yang-based greed. The yin energy is badly needed in this sector. However, the real truth is that many of us want a return to the old ways. As bank shareholders and home owners we want it to be like it was. The truth is that if the financial markets go back to the way they were, then another collapse will be around the next corner. As I heard recently, '3 per cent of the world's population controls 70 per cent of the world's wealth and it has been like this for 5,000 years!'

LOOKING FORWARD

On a more positive note the socio/political-economic system is being exposed as fundamentally flawed and real constructive debate is taking place about the type of world we wish to live in. This is huge progress and we should recognise the relative freedom that we live in in comparison to the times of the Cathars and those who were persecuted for speaking out. Luckily we are on the precipice of spirituality being returned to the communities. Lay people are becoming increasingly important in religious life and are bringing a balance that is slowly but surely making religion more relevant to people in these times of rampant commercialism. In our health system we can see huge improvements, but the greatest thing we now see in health is personal responsibility. Only yesterday I met a man who seven years ago was given three months to live. Of the four major tumours that he was diagnosed with, only one now remains, which is not growing any further. He achieved all this by changing the way he thinks and has not used western medicine except for the purposes of scanning! Inspirational stories such as this are becoming more common and I would like to believe that this is because we nearing a tipping point where our yin and yang will work together to create perfect health.

We have seen during the course of our travels with yin and yang the detrimental effect that we are having on the planet and our environment. Thankfully we are seeing huge efforts by ordinary people to stem the tide of corporate, commercial, yang-based pollution. Very recently I came across an article about Daniel Burd, a Canadian student who has discovered a bacteria that can break down plastic.[64] This could really help decrease the massive amounts of plastic waste worldwide.

Some of you may be aware that in the middle of the Pacific ocean there is a huge whirlpool of tidal currents that draw all debris from around the Pacific into the centre. This area, known as the Pacific garbage patch, which is thousands of miles wide, is dense with plastic packaging and wildlife in the region has been decimated. Because it is in the centre of an ocean we don't see this. The plight has been highlighted by sailors who have sailed in these waters and who were so affected by what they saw they had to take action and start campaigning. The seas are the largest yin aspect in our world, yet we are destroying them with our yang need for cheap consumable and non-recyclable produce.

Water is taken for granted by the western world but what we pollute today we will have to drink tomorrow. I always marvel to think that the water that Jesus drank 2,000 years ago could be the water we drank this morning or washed our cars with. Of all our challenges the healing of our waters represents the greatest one, as we all know water is the source of life.

As we move into the next few years I can see a massive opportunity for balance and a readjustment of the way we live. The current economic crisis may provide us with a vehicle to achieve this, in that we are all aware that even what appears to be the most stable system is in fact unstable. The time we live in now will be a time of great change and advancement of the spirit. Satellite communities grouped according to beliefs and shared values will offer us a real living alternative – an alternative that is powered by new technology (yang) and the ancient ways of balance (yin). This powerful combination of old and new united by positive intention will create a society that recognises and rewards balance.

RIGHT VIEW, RIGHT ACTION

The Dali Lama, the spiritual leader of Tibet and respected Buddhist, counsels that whenever we attempt any changes we should always do so in the context of 'Right View' and 'Right Action'. By this he means that to truly effect the right change we first need to understand what is really happening in the world. In many ways this is the yin – the ability to wait, listen, absorb, empathise, sense and truly see the whole picture. Then and only then, when we are really aware of what is happening, should we turn to the yang or action. Our action should then be the right action, in that it should serve to make the world a better place.

A very simple question I often ask myself and others is: will our action bring light or darkness to people's lives and the world? Often our actions may bring both. For example, advertising a soft drink may bring darkness, in that it may contribute to diabetes and obesity, but on the other hand will bring light in the form of creativity and employment. We are faced with these situations every day. If we consistently make ourselves aware of the implications of our actions then we begin to have a social, environmental and personal consciousness. If you find that your choices bring more darkness than light, it may be time to ask yourself should you really be doing this job? Are you prepared to let your light be compromised by the darkness of greed and reckless profit?

PERSONAL RESPONSIBILITY

By being aware and taking the right action we balance our yin and yang. This leads to the highest form of empowered living which is based on personal responsibility. No longer are we able to say 'that's just the way society is' or 'my company makes that policy not me'. We have to stop hiding and passing our personal responsibility over to others. The truth is that it is easier to let someone else take responsibility and to release our personal power to others. This is no surprise, as for centuries those at the top have used this to control us and through this mechanism obtained power and wealth. As we become self aware as spiritual beings, we realise that each one of us must stand up for our own truth and play our part in a society that can change for the better. When we engage our positive yang energy we push for justice, truth and peace. This understanding of personal responsibility and not shirking the call of destiny has allowed some of the greatest events in history to unfold. As Mahatma Ghandi said, 'my life is my message'.

When we live in our truth, when we allow our masculine and feminine energy to balance, we shine. We inspire others and our light becomes a beacon by which others may find their light, their inner joy, their bliss. This is no longer a choice. It is a prerequisite of this age that we work for light and banish the darkness to history. As Marianne Williamson says in her book a *Return to Love*, 'Our deepest fear is not that we are inadequate. Our deepest fear is that we are powerful beyond measure. It is our light, not our darkness that most frightens us. We ask ourselves, Who am I to be brilliant, gorgeous, talented, fabulous? Actually, who are you *not* to be? You are a child of God. Your playing small does not serve the world.'[65] This is our time. It is up to each and every one of us to embrace our own light, truth, yin and yang.

HOPE AND OPTIMISM

The fuel to get us to the new age must be hope and optimism. Too often the media tells us we are looking down the barrel of a gun. Bad news sells papers. Some people even delight in the misery of their condition. It comes down to choice as to whether we allow the negativity pedalled as part of a greater force of manipulation set on creating fear in the masses, to affect us. We must harden our resolve to the truth even more and make our lives vehicles of optimism and hope. In the end the forces of light, positivity and optimism always win out. As Ekhart Tolle says in *The Power of Now*, 'you cannot find yourself by going into the past. You find yourself by coming into the present.'[66] In this he means that fear and negativity cannot live in the present moment. They are only products of projecting ourselves into the future in the case of fear and living in the past with regret and 'should have, could have thinking'. Rhonda Byrne in *The Secret* counsels, 'the only thing you need to *do* is feel good now'.[67] By living in the now and feeling good about ourselves and our lives right now, we open doors inside ourselves that lead us to the right thing, people and places. Allowing your yin and yang to balance in the now is a key. It is to be effortlessly joyful and positive in every moment. Perhaps the greatest gift we have been given as human beings is the gift of choice. It is up to us to choose our state and our approach to life. Choose your future, choose the balance of your glorious masculine and feminine energies. Choose it now!

Make sure to visit www.brendanfoley.ie to download a free copy of the guided mediation from Chapter 1 – Meet your yin and yang. You can also purchase a full copy of the CD or download all the meditations featured in this book. We also have an ezine you can sign up to and get information about the Yin Yang Complex workshops and news.

Endnotes

1   Norris, Stephanie, *Secrets of Colour Healing* (The Ivy Press Ltd, 2001), p. 13.

2   Jung, C.G. (1964) *Man and His Symbols* (New York, Doubleday and Company).

3   Paddy McCoey, September 2009, *pers. comm.*

4   Wauters, Ambika, *Chakras and their Archetypes* (Crossing Press, 1997).

5   Bruce Bower, *Science News*, 6 July 1985 (Michigan, USA).

6   See www.amatsu.info and see the University of Minnesota for TCM: http://takingcharge.csh.umn.edu/explore-healing-practices/what-traditional-chinese-medicine

7   This is not a medical technique. It is used at the discretion of the reader. The author and publishers accept no liability for any injury caused.

8   George Christos, *Memory and Dreams – The Creative Mind* (Rutgers University Press, 2003), p. 128.

9   Norris, Stephanie, *Secrets of Colour Healing* (London, 2001), p. 15.

10 *Ibid.*

11 Waite, Roger, 'A new study has found the British are the most promiscuous western nation', *Sunday Times*, 30 November 2008.

12 Pope, Marvin H., *Song of Songs* (Anchor Bible series, 1983), p. 19.

13 Aldrete, Gregory S., *Daily Life in the Roman City: Rome, Pompeii and Ostia* (Greenwood Press, 2004), p. 56.

14 Doherty, B. & Valentine, J., *Growing Younger: Age-defying secrets for women* (St Martins Press, 2002), p. 201.

15 www.college-startup.com/college/15-successful-entrepreneurs-who-didnt-need-college/

16 Simmans, Graham, *Jesus after the Crucifixion: from Jerusalem to Rennes-le-Chateau* (Bear & Company, 2007).

17 *Ibid.*, p. 214.

18 Whelan, Dolores, *Ever Ancient, Ever New* (Columba Press, 2006), p. 68.

19 Quoted in Bamford, Christopher, *Celtic Christianity* (Floris Books, Edinburgh, 1986), p. 10. Massingham was a post-Second World War writer who penned many titles about agriculture and the countryside and had a strong historical interest in how local culture had developed and the link of people with the land.

20 Simmans, Graham, *Jesus after the Crucifixion: from Jerusalem to Rennes-le-Chateau* (Bear & Company, 2007), p. 214.

21 Starbird, Margaret, *The Woman with the Alabaster Jar* (Bear & Co., Vermont, 1993).

22 Baigent Michael, Leigh, Richard & Lincoln, Henry, *The Holy Blood and the Holy Grail* (Jonathan Cape, London 1982).

23 Montségur Marie, *Montségur Visitor's Guide* (France), p. 5.

24 *Ibid.*, p. 2

25 Simmans, Graham, *Jesus after the Crucifixion: from Jerusalem to Rennes-le-Chateau* (Bear & Company, 2007), p. 240.

26 Chopra, Deepak, *Ageless Body, Timeless Mind: A practical guide to growing old* (Crown Publishers 1993); Bays, Brandon, *The Journey*

(Thorsons, London 1999); Milner, Kathleen, *Reiki and other rays of healing touch* (Scotsdale AZ, USA 2003); Myss, Caroline, *Anatomy of the Spirit – Seven stages of healing power* (Bantam, 1997); Hay, Louise L., *You Can Heal your Life* (Hay House 1984).

27 Hay, Louise L., *You Can Heal your Life* (Hay House 1984), pp. 220–221.

28 Bays, Brandon, *The Journey* (Thorsons, London 1999).

29 Chopra, Deepak, *Ageless Body, Timeless Mind* (Crown Publishers 1993), p. 6.

30 *Ibid.*

31 Emoto, Masaru, *The Hidden Messages in Water* (Oregon, USA, 2004).

32 Cromie, William J., 'Meditation Changes Temperature', *Harvard University Gazette – Science/Research*, April 2002. http://www.news.harvard.edu/gazette/2002/04.18/09-tummo.html

33 Cromie, William J., 'Meditation increase brain size', *Harvard Science*, Jan 2006. http://www.news.harvard.edu/gazette/daily/2006/01/23-meditation.htmlbrain size

34 Brennan, Barbara Ann, *Hands of Light. A guide to healing through the human energy field* (Bantam, 1988).

35 For more information on chakras please see Wauters, Ambika, *The Book of Chakras – Discover the hidden forces within you* (Quarto Inc, 2002), which is excellent for an overview, and Brennan, Barbara Ann, *Hands of Light. A guide to healing through the human energy field* (Bantam, 1988), which is very detailed and scientific in its approach. I would recommend this for anybody with medical background or training.

36 Myss, Caroline, *Anatomy of the Spirit – Seven stages of healing power* (Bantam, 1997) p. 27.

37 http://www.bbc.co.uk/science/horizon/2003/armageddonqa. shtml; http://news.bbc.co.uk/2/hi/science/nature/645007.stm

38 http://www.nsf.gov/news/special_reports/jellyfish/textonly/ ecology.jsp

39 http://www.peopleandplanet.net/doc.php?id=2784

40 http://www.timesonline.co.uk/tol/news/uk/article492642.ece

41 http://www.earth-policy.org/Transcripts/SenateEPW07. htm for full transcript of briefing to Senate Committee on Environment and Public Works, 13 June 2007.

42 UN and US Census Bureau Figures January 2009.

43 Harrabin, Roger (BBC Environment Analyst) 'Calls To Abandon Bio Fuel Targets', http://news.bbc.co.uk/2/hi/science/ nature/7199073.stm

44 www.guardian.co.uk/lifeandstyle/2008/mar/30/foodanddrink. ethicalliving

45 World Health Organisation, *High Dose Irradiation*, World Health Organisation Technical Report Series, Geneva 1999.

46 Gore, Al, *An Inconvenient Truth* (Paramount, 2006).

47 *Ibid.*

48 Courtesy of http://www.climatecrisis.net.

49 Nickerson, Carol, Schwarz, Norbert, Diener, Ed, Kahneman, Daniel, 'Zeroing in on the dark side of the American Dream: a closer look at the negative consequences of the goal for financial success', *Psychological science: a journal of the American Psychological Society* 14(6), 2003, pp. 531–6.

50 Starbird, Margaret, *The Woman with the Alabaster Jar* (Bear & Company, 1993), p. 25.

51 Starbird, Margaret, *Mary Magdalene: Bride in Exile* (Bear & Company, 2005), p. 152.

52 Stevenson, Ian & Samararatne, Godwin, 'Three New Cases of the Reincarnation Type in Sri Lanka with Written Records Made before Verification', *Journal of Nervous and Mental Disease* 176, 1988, p. 741. For more information see: http://www.healthsystem.virginia.edu/internet/personality studies/home.cfm

53 http://www.brianweiss.com

54 Dowell, William, 'Foreign Exchange: Saddam Turns His Back on Greenbacks', *Time*, Monday 13 Nov., 2000; Islam, Faisal, 'When will we buy oil in euros?', *The Observer*, Sunday 23 February, 2003

55 http://www.liverpoolecho.co.uk/liverpool-news/local-news/ 2009/03/31/dad-of-tim-parry-killed-in-the-warrington-bomb -says-he-can-forgive-but-not-forget-100252-23273144/

56 Andrew Smith, *pers comm.*

57 O'Neill, Andy, *The Power of Charismatic Healing* (Mercier Press, 1985), p. 126.

58 Firth, Niall, 'Human race will split into two different species', *Daily Mail Online*, 26 October 2007. Read more: http:// www.dailymail.co.uk/sciencetech/article-489653/Human-race-split-different-species.html#ixzz0PnM16J6f

59 www.clusterconvention.org

60 Gladwell, Malcolm, *The Tipping Point* (Little, Brown & Co, 2000), pp. 180, 185.

61 US Department of Agriculture, Economic Research Service, US Rice Stocks background information and statistics. http://www.ers.usda.gov/news/ricecoverage.htm

62 http://www.fountain-international.org/origins/cathar.htm

63 http://www.wellesley.edu/Physics/Rberg/glassdemo.html

64 http://news.therecord.com/article/354044

65 Williamson, Marianne, *A Return to Love* (First Harper Perennial, 1993). See also www.marianne.com.

66 Tolle, Ekhart, *The Power of Now* (New World Library, 1999), p. 75.

67 Byrne, Rhonda, *The Secret* (Atria Books, 2006), p. 184.

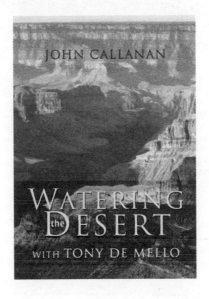

WATERING THE DESERT
John Callanan with Tony de Mello

ISBN: 978 1 85635 444 8

This book is designed for those who try to pray, those who are searching for meaning in their lives and who are prepared to spend a little time in that pursuit.

FINDING FIRE WITH TONY DE MELLO
John Callanan

ISBN: 978 1 85635 343 4

The influence of Anthony de Mello on the lives of those who study him and his teachings is profound. In this book John Callanan attempts to bring de Mello's vitality and energy to a new audience, explaining who Tony de Mello was and why his work was so ground-breaking among Christians. Different types of meditation, fantasy prayer and styles of reflection are described to help the reader to unlock their potential, get their lives into focus and deal with pain and failure.

www.mercierpress.ie

THE LONELY PLANET STORY

The story begins with a classic travel adventure: Tony and Maureen Wheeler's 1972 journey across Europe and Asia to Australia. There was no useful information about the overland trail then, so Tony and Maureen published the first Lonely Planet guidebook to meet a growing need.

From a kitchen table, Lonely Planet has grown to become the largest independent travel publisher in the world, with offices in Melbourne (Australia), Oakland (USA) and London (UK).

Today Lonely Planet guidebooks cover the globe. There is an ever-growing list of books and information in a variety of media. Some things haven't changed. The main aim is still to make it possible for adventurous travellers to get out there – to explore and better understand the world.

At Lonely Planet we believe travellers can make a positive contribution to the countries they visit – if they respect their host communities and spend their money wisely.

SEND US YOUR FEEDBACK

We love to hear from travellers – your comments keep us on our toes and help make our books better. Our well-travelled team reads every word on what you loved or loathed about this book. Although we cannot reply individually to postal submissions, we always guarantee that your feedback goes straight to the appropriate authors, in time for the next edition. Each person who sends us information is thanked in the next edition – and the most useful submissions are rewarded with a free book. See the Behind the Scenes section.

To send us your updates – and find out about Lonely Planet events, newsletters and travel news – visit our award-winning website: **www.lonelyplanet.com/feedback**.

Note: We may edit, reproduce and incorporate your comments in Lonely Planet products such as guidebooks, websites and digital products, so let us know if you don't want your comments reproduced or your name acknowledged. For a copy of our privacy policy, go to www.lonelyplanet .com/privacy.

Published by Lonely Planet Publications Pty Ltd

ABN 36 005 607 983

© Lonely Planet 2005

© photographers as indicated 2005

Cover photographs: Sweden, Lapland, illuminated cabin in snow under Aurora Borealis, Peter Lilja/Getty Images (front); The canals of Copenhagen, Denmark, Ned Friary/Lonely Planet Images (back). Many of the images in this guide are available for licensing from Lonely Planet Images: www.lonelyplanetimages.com

Printed through The Bookmaker International Ltd
Printed in China

LONELY PLANET OFFICES

Australia
Head Office
Locked Bag 1, Footscray, Victoria 3011
☎ 03 8379 8000, fax 03 8379 8111
talk2us@lonelyplanet.com.au

USA
150 Linden St, Oakland, CA 94607
☎ 510 893 8555, toll free 800 275 8555
fax 510 893 8572, info@lonelyplanet.com

UK
72–82 Rosebery Ave,
Clerkenwell, London EC1R 4RW
☎ 020 7841 9000, fax 020 7841 9001
go@lonelyplanet.co.uk